Praise for *Teach You*

"Archimedes said, 'Give me a lever long enough and a fulcrum on which to place it, and I will move the world.' Students' willingness to work hard—and students will work hard if the work is worth it—is the lever. Dr. McGuire's practical strategies are the fulcrum. Hard work plus bad strategies gets you almost nowhere. But hard work plus *effective* strategies? You can go out and change the world with what you learn!"—*Victoria Bhavsar, Director of the Faculty Center for Professional Development and the eLearning Team, California State Polytechnic University, Pomona*

"McGuire hits it out of the park with this book written for students. She easily connects to them through her conversational style, empathy, case studies and a strong belief in their power to succeed. She shares strategies for learning through graphics and activities that ensure their active engagement. She fully understands the importance of readability as she fills the text with questions. This book explodes with energy and passion and should be on every student's bookshelf."—*Martha E. Casazza, Educational Consultant, TRPPAssociates, CLADEA Founding Fellow*

"Time and time again, I brought Dr. McGuire to several historically Black colleges and universities, such as Johnson C. Smith University, Dillard University, Cheyney University, and Bennett College, to expose students and faculty to proven strategies, as described in this book, that students can use to teach themselves 'how to learn.' I also shared these strategies with my daughter and her friends while they were in medical school at East Carolina University. Simply put, these strategies work!"—*Phyllis Worthy Dawkins, President, Bennett College*

"Dr. McGuire has extended her expertise directly to students in this companion to *Teach Students How to Learn*. After impacting faculty and academic support professionals' approach to helping students learn best, she now introduces and guides students to deeper understanding of concepts at different levels. By reframing their approach to studying in college using her methods, they can become better motivated, manage their study time effectively, earn higher grades, and develop successful college careers." —*Johanna Dvorak, Director Emerita, Educational Support Services, University of Wisconsin-Milwaukee, Educational Research Consulting, LLC.*

"*Teach Yourself How to Learn* can be a life changer. With this book, students will gain the insights and concrete techniques that are the foundations of effective learning and studying. No less important, the book is written so that students will want to read it. The information is conveyed without jargon and in a style that relates to students' experiences. I believe that students who read this book will be able to optimize their educational experiences and become enthusiastic and effective life-long learners." —*Mark McDaniel, Center for Integrative Research on Cognition, Learning, and Education, Washington University in St. Louis; and coauthor of* Make It Stick: The Science of Successful Learning

"This book is going to help so many students!!! Dr. McGuire is a master storyteller armed with the science of learning. From each chapter to the next, strategies are strategically laid out in a way to help any learner in any course. Read one chapter or the entire book, and if you follow the suggestions provided you will see a difference in not only what you learn but also, more importantly, how you think about learning." —*Todd Zakrajsek, Associate Professor, Department of Family Medicine; and Executive Director of the Academy of Educators in the School of Medicine, University of North Carolina at Chapel Hill*

TEACH YOURSELF HOW TO LEARN

creating
evaluating
analyzing
applying
understanding
remembering

TEACH YOURSELF HOW TO LEARN

Strategies You Can Use to Ace Any Course
at Any Level

Saundra Yancy McGuire
with Stephanie McGuire

Foreword by Mark McDaniel

Routledge
Taylor & Francis Group

NEW YORK AND LONDON

First published in 2018 by Stylus Publishing, LLC.

Published in 2023 by Routledge
605 Third Avenue, New York, NY 10017
4 Park Square, Milton Park, Abingdon, Oxon OX14 4RN

Routledge is an imprint of the Taylor & Francis Group, an informa business.

© 2018 Taylor & Francis Group

Notice:
Product or corporate names may be trademarks or registered trademarks, and are used only for identification and explanation without intent to infringe.

Library of Congress Cataloging-in-Publication Data
Names: McGuire, Saundra Yancy, author. |
McGuire, Stephanie, author.
Title: Teach yourself how to learn strategies you can use to ace any course at any level / Saundra Yancy McGuire with Stephanie McGuire ; foreword by Mark McDaniel.
Description: First edition. |
Sterling, Virginia : Stylus Publishing, LLC., [2018] |
Includes bibliographical references and index.
Identifiers: LCCN 2017026863
ISBN 9781620367551 (cloth : alk. paper) |
ISBN 9781620367568 (pbk. : alk. paper) |
Subjects: LCSH: Learning, Psychology of. | Study skills. | Motivation in education. | Metacognition.
LCC LB1060 .M385 2018 (print) |
DDC 370.15--dc23
LC record available at https://lccn.loc.gov/2017026863

ISBN: 978-1-62036-755-1 (hbk)
ISBN: 978-1-62036-756-8 (pbk)
ISBN: 978-1-00344-732-0 (ebk)

DOI: 10.4324/9781003447320

To my grandchildren, Joshua, Ruth, Daniel, and Joseph, whose pursuit of academic excellence continues the endeavors of preceding generations and honors the legacy of their great-great grandmother, Effie Jane Gordon Yancy.

CONTENTS

FOREWORD   *ix*
Mark McDaniel

ACKNOWLEDGMENTS   *xiii*

INTRODUCTION   *1*

1   MY JOURNEY
I Was Once In Your Shoes   *3*

2   WHY DON'T ALL STUDENTS ALREADY KNOW HOW TO
LEARN?   *6*

3   METACOGNITION
What It Is and How It Can Turbocharge Your Learning   *9*

4   THE POWER OF BLOOM'S TAXONOMY AND THE STUDY
CYCLE   *23*

5   METACOGNITIVE LEARNING STRATEGIES AT WORK   *40*

6   WHY YOUR MINDSET ABOUT INTELLIGENCE MATTERS   *59*

7   HOW YOUR EMOTIONS AFFECT YOUR MOTIVATION AND
LEARNING   *73*

8   WHAT YOU CAN DO TO BOOST YOUR MOTIVATION,
POSITIVE EMOTIONS, AND LEARNING   *82*

Contents

9   TIME MANAGEMENT, TEST TAKING, AND
    STRESS REDUCTION   *89*

10 TRY THE STRATEGIES AND HAVE FUN!   *100*

APPENDIX A
Compilation of Strategies for Students   *105*

APPENDIX B
Books and Links Recommended for Students   *108*

APPENDIX C
Learning Strategies Inventory   *109*

APPENDIX D
Dramatic Individual Student Improvement   *111*

APPENDIX E
Selected Student Feedback   *113*

APPENDIX F
Study Tools   *123*

REFERENCES   *127*

ABOUT THE AUTHORS   *131*

INDEX   *133*

FOREWORD

In many ways, this is an exciting time to be a student. A plethora of engaging materials are available to stimulate students' thinking and to capture their interest. Elementary and middle school students can learn about radiocarbon dating by reading comic book narratives (Hunt & Swogger, n.d.). To learn neuroscience, more advanced students can interact with *Betty's Brain* (a computer program in which a student teaches "Betty" about her brain and then poses questions to determine if Betty accurately understands the neuroscience concepts the student is trying to teach; Leelawong & Biswas, 2008). College students can enroll in flipped classrooms in which cooperative learning occurs in small discussion groups within the context of a larger class (e.g., Talanquer & Pollard, 2010). Moreover, teachers at every educational level are becoming familiar with and adjusting their instruction to align with the scientific principles of learning.

Yet, being a student may also be more challenging than it has ever been. Curricula for sciences and social sciences continue to expand as more and more critical information is added to the knowledge base, a knowledge base that educators feel compelled to cover in their courses. In this environment, one often hears students complain that their courses are crammed with information that they are expected to memorize, learn, and master. The essence of the situation, then, is this: Teachers are working hard to design state-of-the-art courses, based on the best available learning-sciences evidence. But once the student leaves the classroom, he or she is largely responsible for figuring out how to learn all of the information presented in class. The current state of affairs is that teachers focus on teaching content—on *what* students need to learn—and not on teaching *how* students should go about learning (Dunlosky, 2013).

From my perspective, this state of affairs reflects a seriously flawed assumption, an assumption that is implicit in our educational system. The assumption is that students (humans) know how to learn. In fact, numerous published surveys of students' learning and study strategies from middle school to college clearly indicate that students typically embrace and practice ineffective learning and study techniques. Further, an abundance of evidence from the sciences of learning indicates that students' beliefs about which study conditions lead to the best learning outcomes are often in direct opposition to the actual learning outcomes. Without question, and this is the premise of *Teach Yourself How to Learn*, many students do not know how to learn.

The upshot is that the current educational milieu is a grand paradox. Educators demand that students learn an incredible amount of material, but at the same time most educators do not provide students with the skills—with the "toolkit"—to accomplish that enormous task. This is like throwing a child with no swimming skills in the deep end of the swimming pool and demanding that the child *swim*. We would never do this, because we would expect that many children would not survive. But in education, often we do exactly this; we throw material at students, many with poor learning skills, and insist that they learn. Some students do figure out how to learn, but many do not. Even a large percentage of post-secondary students endorse the following statement: "Often, I feel I'm drowning in the sheer amount of material with which I have to cope" (Bunce et al., in press). A fair number of students are drowning in their courses, and they are drowning in our educational system.

It is in this context that *Teach Yourself How to Learn* can be a life changer. This book provides you with a toolkit for learning. It describes reliable and evidence-based techniques that you can easily adopt. You will learn about diagnosing any shortcomings in your own study techniques. To shore up those shortcomings, you will learn about effective ways to learn and build understanding. You will discover how to increase comprehension of reading assignments by taking steps to engage in active reading, to increase understanding by posing and answering deep level questions, and to increase learning by studying as if you were going to teach the assigned material to the class. With this book, you will gain the insights and concrete techniques that are the foundations of effective learning and studying.

No less important, this book is written without jargon and in a style that relates to your experiences. I believe you will find that this book will optimize your educational experiences and place you on the path to being an enthusiastic and effective life-long learner.

Mark McDaniel
Codirector,
Center for Integrative Research on Cognition,
Learning, and Education (CIRCLE),
Washington University in St. Louis;
Coauthor of *Make It Stick: The Science of Successful Learning*

ACKNOWLEDGMENTS

Writing this book has been a labor of love, and I have many individuals and groups to thank for their contributions. First and foremost, I must thank Sarah Baird, the wonderful learning strategist who introduced me to the idea that we could teach students how to become better learners, and who showed me how to do it. Her workshops were paradigm-shifting experiences for me, as she demonstrated just how to teach students effective strategies, make them believe in their ability to excel, and motivate them to change their behavior. And I thank my colleagues at the Louisiana State University (LSU) Center for Academic Success (CAS), especially Melissa Brocato, Pam Ball, Diane Mohler, Nanette Cheatham, Susan Saale, Dr. Erin Wheeler, Christy O'Neal, and Naresh Sonti for actively participating in a collaborative effort to teach students effective learning strategies. Very special thanks go to Lisa Gullett, the CAS office manager who not only developed systems to help keep track of the thousands of students who used the center but also kept us sane when we were juggling too many projects at once. Thanks also go to Dean Carolyn Collins and Dr. Rhonda Atkinson for establishing the LSU learning center and developing it into the outstanding unit that it was when I came to LSU in 1999.

Since 1999 I have attended many workshops and faculty development sessions that have helped to develop and shape the ideas presented in this book. The organizations that I thank for providing particularly insightful sessions and access to immensely helpful mentors are the National College Learning Center Association (NCLCA), the College Reading & Learning Association (CRLA), the Professional and Organizational Development (POD) Network, and the Southern Association of Colleges and Schools Commission on Colleges (SACSCOC). Several individuals from these organizations have been invaluable mentors to me. Chief among them was the late and inestimable Dr. Frank L. Christ; Dr. Russ Hodges, Dr. Karen Agee, and Dr. Dee Fink have also given me indispensable guidance and support.

I sincerely thank the thousands of students who used the strategies and who dispelled my initial skepticism about their effectiveness. These students had enough faith in me and my colleagues to try the approaches we were suggesting, even though they may have had their doubts about whether those changes would make a difference. And I thank them for sharing the strategies with their friends when their grades began to soar. In particular, I would like to thank David Hall, whose feedback regarding the first incarnation of this book, *Teach Students How to Learn* (McGuire, 2015), inspired me to produce a version for students. The furiously enthusiastic way he absorbed and applied concepts presented for an audience of instructors convinced me that a student edition would be essential.

Sincere thanks also go to my friend Dr. Roald Hoffmann for inviting me to coauthor articles about teaching learning strategies in *Science* and the *American Scientist*. These accounts allowed me to spread the word to a much wider audience. And I extend special thanks to my friend Dr. Isiah Warner and the staff of the LSU Office of Strategic Initiatives (OSI). They incorporated the strategies into programs offered to students in OSI programs and obtained funding to provide the information to more students. Dr. Evanna Gleason should also be acknowledged for the invaluable feedback and guidance she gave regarding the neurobiology of stress, memory, and learning.

We express our heartfelt thanks to Melissa Bailey Crawford for her careful and insightful comparative review of our earlier work, *Teach Students How to Learn*, and a final draft of this book. Her comments and suggestions for improvement were invaluable.

We owe a huge debt of gratitude to John von Knorring, president of Stylus Publishing, for his unflagging support and encouragement to write this book for students after we informed him of the very positive feedback we were receiving from students who had read the faculty version. We also want to wholeheartedly thank Alexandra Hartnett, managing production editor, and the other members of the Stylus group, including Teresa Lewandowski, who produced this text in record time.

Designer Kathleen Dyson also deserves heartfelt acknowledgment for her gorgeous cover art. We deeply appreciate Patricia Webb and Arlene Aiello for their indispensable marketing and administrative support, respectively.

My sincere and boundless gratitude goes to Dr. Mark McDaniel, coauthor of *Make It Stick: The Science of Successful Learning* (Brown, Roediger, & McDaniel, 2014), for readily accepting my request to write the foreword. As a cognitive psychologist, he has a unique perspective on how the findings of cognitive science can be translated into specific strategies that will improve student learning.

I also want to acknowledge and thank my wonderful family. I was blessed to be born into a family of educators. My grandmother, Mrs. Effie Jane Gordon Yancy; my parents, Mr. and Mrs. Robert (Delsie) Yancy Jr.; and most of my aunts and uncles were outstanding educators who inspired their students to excel. Special thanks also go to my brothers, Robert Yancy III and Dr. Eric A. Yancy, who have both served as sounding boards for many of the ideas presented here. I extend deep appreciation to my sister, Annette L. Yancy, an academic adviser at LSU who was recognized as the 2012 National Advisor of the Year by the National Academic Advising Association. She has taught learning strategies to many of her students during advising sessions, demonstrating that staff as well as faculty can teach students how to learn.

I am most grateful for the unwavering support, encouragement, guidance, and inspiration that my husband, Dr. Stephen C. McGuire, the love of my life, has provided throughout the almost five decades of our marriage, and—more specifically—during the process of completing this book. When we met as first-year college students at Southern University in Baton Rouge, Louisiana, he was already using metacognitive learning strategies—even before the label was coined! And I offer sincere thanks to our daughters, Dr. Carla McGuire Davis and Dr. Stephanie McGuire, and to our grandchildren, Joshua, Ruth, Daniel, and Joseph Davis. All of them have been willing subjects as I used them to test the effectiveness of many of the strategies presented here.

There are no words to convey my gratitude for my coauthor and daughter, Dr. Stephanie McGuire. She provided valuable insights and suggestions about the content of this book, and she created most of the text for this book. I can unequivocally state that this book would not exist were it not for her collaboration on the project.

If we have left anyone out, please accept our apologies and know that we thank you too. Producing this book has been a community effort, and we are truly grateful for the part that everyone played in its development.

INTRODUCTION

Comeback Kids

Miriam, a freshman calculus student at Louisiana State University (LSU), made 37.5% on her first exam but 83% and 93% on the next two exams. Robert, a first-year general chemistry student at LSU, made 42% on his first exam and followed that up with three 100%s in a row. Matt, a first-year general chemistry student at the University of Utah, scored 65% and 55% on his first two exams and 95% on his third exam. I could go on. I could tell you scores of stories like this from the last 15 years of my teaching career.

Something happened to all of these students between their last failing grade and their first good grade. They learned something new.

No Miracles, Just Strategies

Recently I was talking to a colleague who had heard about these remarkable transformations. She exclaimed, "You're a miracle worker! I want to be a miracle worker, too!" I quickly told her that there was really nothing magical about the surges in students' test scores after I worked with them; hundreds of faculty and learning center professionals are getting these same results on campuses around the country. But there are tens of thousands of faculty members, like my colleague, as well as hundreds of thousands of students, who don't know what some students are doing to bring about their seemingly miraculous results.

I wrote this book to let everyone in on one of the best-kept secrets in education: Any student can use simple, straightforward strategies to start making As in his or her courses and enjoy a lifetime of deep, effective learning.

From Skeptic to Convert

When I first encountered some of these learning strategies, at LSU's Center for Academic Success (CAS), I was skeptical. The strategies seemed too straightforward and simple to make a difference, and I didn't think students would use them. But after I began to see students who had been making Ds and Fs turn into straight-A students, I became convinced that these simple tools work miracles.

If you find yourself feeling skeptical that these strategies will work, I implore you to use them for just three weeks. What have you got to lose?

My Promise to You

By the time you finish this book you will

- understand why you may not know how to learn;
- have concrete, effective learning strategies to try;
- know how to change your mindset about intelligence and increase your motivation; and
- have everything you need to make As in your courses!

I

MY JOURNEY

I Was Once In Your Shoes

I Get It

Let me say a little bit about why I have so much compassion for students. Confession time: Throughout my undergraduate career, I almost never studied until the night before an exam. I love to tell the following story, which illustrates my cluelessness in full Technicolor. One day, during my senior year at Southern University in Baton Rouge, I was walking down the hall with one of my favorite chemistry professors, Jack Jefferson. Dr. Jefferson asked me a question about a basic chemical reaction, and I breezily replied that I had no idea how to answer his question, feeling absolutely no shame about my ignorance. At that time, I had no learning goals.

Another story: After graduation, I headed to Cornell to pursue my graduate degree in chemistry, and I knew that when I arrived, I would have to take placement exams in general, organic, analytical, and physical chemistry. So I arrived in Ithaca a week early and set myself on a crash memorization course. I passed all my exams and was given a full load of graduate courses. I don't know why it didn't occur to me that if I passed the placement exams the subsequent courses I took would require mastery of all the content I'd just tried to force-feed my brain!

I continued my practice of cramming the night before an exam and began to make lower grades in my courses than I ever had in my life. I decided to visit one of my professors, Mel Goldstein, to discuss my grades. Dr. Goldstein gave weekly homework assignments but made them optional. Of course, I never tried to do them until the night before the test. But at that point, I had nowhere near enough time to figure out the problems, so I would give up and go back to rote memorization. During our chat in his office, Dr. Goldstein told me that he was surprised my grades weren't worse, given that I never did the homework. Then he asked me why I never did it. The question caught me by surprise, so I lied and said that I did the homework but didn't turn it in because it was optional. (I'm pretty sure he knew I wasn't telling the truth.) It had never occurred to me that doing nonrequired homework would help me learn the material and improve my performance on tests! Instead of seeing the relationship between effort and performance, I began to think, "If I can't make As in these courses by doing what I've always done to make As, chemistry must not be what I was meant to do."

Although I was at Cornell on a full Danforth Foundation fellowship, I was still required to teach because Cornell views teaching as crucial to its graduate students' intellectual and professional development. That requirement turned out to be my saving grace. I was given one section of introductory chemistry as a teaching assistant, and I instantly fell in love with teaching. I had never taught before, but very quickly I saw that I was effective. My success with students was addictive because I loved seeing that "aha!" moment on their faces. They would come to me in a fog of confusion, convinced that chemistry would be impossible to learn. But when I helped them understand the logic of the discipline, introduced them to a systematic way to approach the material, and expressed confidence in their intellectual abilities, they suddenly began to understand and instantly became motivated to spend time mastering the material themselves. I found, and still find, student transformation intoxicating. And I am convinced that every learner can personally experience it.

In sum, because I found teaching so exciting, I decided to pursue a master's degree in chemical education and have never looked back. I'm happy to report that, thanks to the learning strategies I acquired along the way, I never earned a grade lower than A in any of my chemistry or education courses for the rest of my graduate career. And today, I know exactly what I would say to myself in 1970 to earn all As in my Cornell graduate chemistry courses!

Good News

The good news is that anyone can undergo the same transformation that I did. I freely admit that I was clueless. If I changed, you can too. You can learn simple strategies that will boost your grades and make learning more fun than you ever thought it could be.

Questions to Ask Yourself

1. Can you relate to the author's experience? If so, how? If not, why?
2. Do you believe your current academic performance is related more to your ability or the amount of effort you are putting into your courses?
3. Do you believe you can undergo the same change as the author?

2

WHY DON'T ALL STUDENTS ALREADY KNOW HOW TO LEARN?

"What did most of your teachers in high school do the class period before the test?"
"They gave us a review."
"What did they do during the review?"
"They told us what questions were going to be on the test and gave us the answers."

onsider some interesting statistics. The Higher Education Research Institute (HERI) published a study in 2017 that revealed that 56.0% of fall 2016 incoming freshmen reported spending *fewer than 6 hours per week* doing homework in 12th grade (Eagan et al., 2017, p. 47), but 92.5% of survey participants said that they graduated from high school with an A or B average (Eagan et al., 2017, p. 31). These statistics demonstrate that for many students, doing the focused, joyful work of deep learning has not been required for good grades.

Presumably because of their grades, these students are also extremely confident; 72.6% of them believe their academic ability is above average or in the highest 10% among people their age (Eagan et al., 2017, p. 49). So, many of you are not only accustomed to successfully breezing

Figure 2.1. Why Many Students Do Not Know How to Learn

- They did not *need* to learn in order to make As and Bs in high school.

- They believe they are in at least the top half of students their age, unaware that they can become smarter.

Note. Data from HERI support the idea that many students do not know how to learn because they are overconfident and academically successful without much effort (Eagan et al., 2017).

through school but also unaware that horizons of learning and success exist beyond those you have already encountered (Figure 2.1).

Okay, So High School Was Easy. Why Don't Some Students Heed Warnings About What They Need to Do in College?

One struggling math major from rural Louisiana on a full scholarship at LSU explained,

> People told me that college was going to require a lot more of my time and effort, but I didn't believe them because I had heard it before. They said that high school was going to be a lot more difficult than middle school, but it wasn't. And when I went to middle school, they had told me it was going to be much harder than elementary school. But I didn't find that at all.

So this young man, along with the other 72.6% of students who judge themselves to be above average compared to their peers (Eagan et al., 2017), very reasonably did not imagine that the typical warnings about a college workload applied to him.

Students are often told that they need to change their habits and do something different when they go to the next level of education, whether high school, college, graduate school, or professional school. But that's like saying, "When you go to another planet next month, you've got to breathe differently." It's not your fault that you may not know what to do to be successful in a more challenging academic environment. Thankfully, there's a way to learn how to breathe differently—how to engage in deep, satisfying learning.

Questions to Ask Yourself

1. Discuss how easy or difficult you found homework, papers, quizzes, and exams at your previous level of education (e.g., middle school, high school, college, or beyond). Is the learning more difficult at your current level of education? If so, in what ways?

2. How is your current learning experience different, if at all, from your previous level of education (e.g., middle school, high school, undergrad)?

3

METACOGNITION

What It Is and How It Can Turbocharge Your Learning

"I have tried the suggestions you gave . . . and it was like magic, seriously."

—Matt J., junior, Department of Microbiology at Weber State University, personal communication, September 15, 2014

In this chapter, we investigate the overarching principle that enables students to stop failing their classes and start acing them: metacognition. We also get our first taste of how learning strategies can dramatically improve performance.

First, we learn what metacognition is and how it helped two students increase their exam scores by at least 30 points. Second, I ask you to do a brief exercise that demonstrates the huge difference that learning strategies can make. Finally, we discuss why these strategies make such an impact and enable you to take charge of your own learning.

A Tale of Two Students

Figure 3.1 shows the dramatic improvement of two students after learning about metacognition. Some faculty in my workshops have thought that these students are fictional, but I assure you they are as real as you and I. Have I got your attention?

9

Figure 3.1. A Tale of Two Students

Exam scores showing rapid and dramatic progress of two LSU
students after they learned metacognitive strategies

Travis, third-year psychology student
47, 52, **82, 86**

Dana, first-year physics student
80, 54, **91, 97, 90** (final exam)

Note. Figure 3.1 shows the exam scores of two students before (plain text) and after (bold text) being exposed to metacognitive strategies. Travis received a B in Introductory Psychology, and Dana received an A in General Physics.

Before we learn more about Travis and Dana, let's investigate what metacognition means.

What Is Metacognition?

Metacognition, a term coined by John H. Flavell (1976), is *thinking about your own thinking*.[1] It's like you have a big brain outside of your brain looking at what your brain is doing. Aspects of Flavell's definition of *metacognition* appear in Figure 3.2.

When you use metacognition, you become consciously aware of yourself as a problem solver, which enables you to actively seek solutions to any problems you may encounter, rather than relying on others to tell you what to do or to answer your questions. As you make the transition from being a passive student to being a proactive learner, you will gain the ability to monitor, plan, and control your mental processing. In other words, instead of staggering through a maze, using instinct alone to look for cheese, you will become aware that you need to plot a course and search systematically for cheese, keeping track of what works and what doesn't. Metacognition also gives you the ability to accurately judge how deeply you have learned something, whether you have only a superficial understanding or the ability to widely apply your knowledge. For example, while studying, you might start to ask

Figure 3.2. Metacognition

The ability to:

• think about your own thinking

• be consciously aware of yourself as a problem solver

• monitor, plan, and control your mental processing

• accurately judge your level of learning

Note. Figure 3.2 shows four aspects of John Flavell's (1976) definition of *metacognition.*

yourself, "Am I understanding this material, or just memorizing it?" When you use metacognition, you become tremendously empowered as a learner because you begin to be able to teach yourself.

Metacognition, Schmetacognition, I Just Need to Work Harder

How do I know that you need metacognition, that you aren't already aware of yourself as a problem solver and are simply not working hard enough? I wonder whether the following scenario has ever happened to you. You excitedly turn in an exam, an essay, or a research paper, beaming with pride, knowing that you've done a great job. Then when you get it back, it's covered with red ink with a big "C" at the top, or worse, a "D" or an "F."

When your work is returned to you with a much lower grade than expected, it's understandably difficult for you to process the cognitive dissonance. You believed you were smart and competent. Does this grade mean you are dumb and incapable? Of course it doesn't, but your doubts are already active. You begin withdrawing psychologically; you might sit back farther in the classroom or lecture hall; worse, you might start missing class. Then your performance on the next test is worse than your performance on the first. The downward spiral continues until you've flunked the course or barely passed it.

If this has ever happened to you, then clearly you were not able to accurately judge your own learning. And the discouragement of thwarted expectations *prevented* you from working harder. Moreover, even if in such situations you are able to rally and work harder, doing more of what you already know how to do is not likely to help. You need to learn a different way. When you learn about metacognition and implement metacognitive strategies, your performance will turn around. Let's see how well metacognition worked for Travis and Dana.

Travis, Psychology Student

Travis was a junior I started working with only the night before his third introductory psychology exam. He had made scores of 47 and 52 on the first two exams, and we spoke for about 30 minutes via telephone because Travis's schedule didn't allow time for us to meet in person. Travis called me after his test was returned to say he had made an 82! I was quite surprised because I had thought he would score in the low to mid-70s. I kept my surprise to myself and said, "That's fantastic, Travis! Okay, if you make higher than a"—racking my brain for a stretch score that would probably be just out of reach for him—"than an 85 on the next test, I will take you to lunch." Mind you, at that point in my journey with metacognition, I did not expect Travis to score higher than 85. In fact, I thought that his 82 was a fluke. These days, I know that when students use metacognition, the sky is the limit. Wouldn't you know, Travis called me back about three weeks later and said, "Dr. McGuire, I made an 86 on that test!" I started looking forward to lunch because I wanted to find out exactly how Travis had done so well. During our meal, I asked Travis, "What are you doing to earn these fabulous grades?" And he replied, "I'm just doing that stuff you told me to do." We'll see in chapter 5 exactly which metacognitive strategies made the difference for Travis.

Dana, Physics Student

Dana was a freshman physics major who had come to LSU supported by a prestigious American Physical Society scholarship, but we met for the first time at a Change Your Major workshop. Dana was trying to get out of physics. Even though she'd wanted to be a medical physicist since the beginning of her junior year in high school, she had become demoralized after making an 80 and a 54 on her first two general physics exams. In high school, she had been a straight-A student, so when she saw 54 at the top of an exam paper, she thought, "Okay, I'm outta here."

At the Change Your Major workshop, Dana introduced herself. "Hi, my name is Dana. I was a physics major, but I'm having trouble, so I need to find something else." The counselor replied, "Oh, yeah, I understand. Physics is haaaard. We will find you something you can do."

I raised an eyebrow and chuckled to myself.

As Dana was leaving, I called her aside and asked, "Dana, do you have an hour to meet with me in my office?" She readily agreed, and I said to her, "Dana, I'm not going to try to talk you out of leaving physics, because if you really want to do something else, that's fine with me, but I want you to know that if you leave physics, it's not because you can't do physics. It's because you've chosen to do something else."

So Dana came to my office, and we talked for about an hour. She made a 91 on the next test, a 97 on the one after, and a 90 on the final exam. She received an A in her general physics course and a 4.0 that semester. Even though her next semester involved illness and two hospital stays, Dana still earned a 3.2 GPA. She graduated in 2012 with a 3.8 GPA in physics, and in the summer of 2014 she graduated with a master's degree in medical physics from the world-renowned University of Texas MD Anderson Cancer Center. Metacognition can give students back their hopes and dreams. We'll discover in chapter 5 which metacognitive strategies Dana used to make her grades soar.

You Can Do It, I Promise

Even if you have experienced abject failure, all is not lost. I often share with new students the dramatic successes of previous students like Travis and Dana so that they can see what is possible. I say to them, "I don't care if you made a 2% on the first test. I know that you have the ability to make a 100% on the next test because your score on the first test is not any indication of how smart you are. It's a reflection of your behaviors, the way you prepared for the first test. And I can teach you a way to prepare that's going to help you ace the next test."

An Exercise for You: Count the Vowels

Now you're going to do an exercise I often do in my student and faculty workshops. Even if you've seen it before, take a moment to refamiliarize yourself with it. You'll need a few things to do this exercise:

- Timer or stopwatch (most smartphones have them, but a watch with a second hand will also work)
- A piece of paper to cover the opposing page once you turn over page 15 and start the exercise
- A pen or pencil

Once you've collected these supplies, set your timer for 45 seconds. When you press start, you're going to do three things: (a) turn page 15 over, (b) cover the opposing page with a piece of paper, and (c) count all of the vowels in the text of Figure 3.3 on page 16 until time runs out. Ready, set, go!

Turn the page for Figure 3.3.

Figure 3.3. Count the Vowels

Dollar bill	Cat lives
Dice	Bowling pins
Tricycle	Football team
Four-leaf clover	Dozen eggs
Hand	Unlucky Friday
Six-pack	Valentine's Day
Seven-Up	Quarter hour
Octopus	

After time is up, or whenever you've finished counting the vowels, immediately cover up the text and reveal the opposing page for your next instructions.

How did it go? Now close your eyes and try to recall all of the words and phrases that you just saw. List as many as you can in the blanks.

football   team

Cat lives

Now look at the original list, and write down the number of items you were able to accurately remember here: __2__. Divide that number by 15, multiply by 100, and that's your score as a percentage. How did you do? C? D? F?

Typically, when I do this in workshops, the average number of correct responses is 3, or 20%, so most workshop groups start out with a spectacularly failing grade. Let's call it F minus.

Now look at the list in Figure 3.3 again, reading each column from top to bottom, and see if you can figure out the underlying organizing principle. Take no more than 10 to 15 seconds to see if you can work it out. If after 10 to 15 seconds you are still unsure, turn this page, and read the top two lines on page 18 before turning back to this page and finishing the following instructions.

Set your timer again for 45 seconds, and this time, study the list and try to commit all 15 phrases to memory. When time is up, turn the page and list as many items as you can remember.

The list is organized according to number. Dollar bill corresponds to the number 1, dice corresponds to 2, tricycle corresponds to 3, and so forth.

dollar bill	1		cat lives	8
dice	2		bowling pins	9
tricicle	3		football team	10
four-leaf clover	4			
hand	5		unlucky friday	11
six-pack	6		valentines day	12
seven up	7		quarter hour	13

Again, look at the original list, and write down the number of items you were able to accurately remember here: __13__. Divide that number by 15, multiply by 100, and that's your new score as a percentage. How did you do this time? A? B? C?

Typically, in workshops, the average number of correct responses for this part of the exercise is 12, or 80%, with many participants achieving 100%! Just as they can go from 20% to 100%, so can you.

Count the Vowels: What Made the Difference?

Obviously, between our first and second attempts to recall the list, we had not become any smarter. So what made the difference? Two things. Before you read further, try to figure out the two differences that made better performance possible.

First, we were aware of our goal. We knew that we needed to memorize the list instead of count the vowels. How does that pertain to your classes? Faculty will often give assignments such as, "Read chapter 1." Many students unknowingly interpret that assignment as, "I should skim chapter 1 while scrolling through Facebook, getting caught up on Instagram, checking out the newest Snapchat filter, and WhatsApping my bestie."

When I was in college and my professors gave me problem sets, I genuinely believed that my objective was to turn in correct solutions for all of the problems. Not until I began teaching did I realize that my college professors were actually more interested in how I solved the problems than in my final answers. They wanted me to understand the *concepts* relevant to each problem and to be able to apply those concepts to new contexts. Just as I totally missed that important point, you may be missing it too.

A brief, related word about practice tests: When professors give practice tests, students often think their goal should be to answer those specific questions. So they spend time memorizing specific information or problem-solving procedures required only for questions on the practice test. Well-intentioned instructors often give the practice tests without the answers, explaining to students that they should come talk to the instructor if they have questions. To their credit, these instructors are sincerely trying to prevent students from sidestepping meaningful learning. Unfortunately, though, the students usually just take the practice tests to the campus learning center or tutorial center and ask the professionals there to show them exactly how to answer the questions or do the problems.

The take-home message here is that many students can be very goal oriented and so focused on grades that they unintentionally avoid real learning. To correct for this tendency, you must give yourself precise goals and tasks, even if your instructor does not. You can use metacognition to take a vague instruction like, "Read chapter 5" and break it down into parts like, "Apply reading strategy to each section of chapter 5; Review notes; Give mini-lecture to empty chairs or best friend; Create practice quiz."

What was the second difference between our two attempts to remember the phrases in the Count the Vowels exercise? We had a very good system for learning the information. Notice the two aspects of that statement: We had not just a system—a way to recognize how the information was organized—but a *very good* system. What made it very good? We related the information to something very familiar to us—in this case, numbers. It is a basic learning principle that whenever the brain is trying to absorb something new, it tries to relate new information to something it already knows (Gregory & Parry, 2006).

From Finding Fault to Accepting Responsibility

When students learn about metacognition, gain learning strategies, and become active learners, it empowers them tremendously because they begin to understand that thinking and learning are processes that *they* can control.

My colleagues (Zhao, Wardeska, McGuire, & Cook, 2014) asked a group of students who had not learned about metacognition to give reasons for their lackluster performance on their first exam in a chemistry course. Take a look at their answers:

I studied but blanked out during [the] exam. I thought I knew it but I didn't. It made perfect sense on [the] board [during the lecture], but not when I did it [in the exam]. I couldn't figure out why I didn't know it. (p. 51)

There were not examples of problems like the ones on the test. I have never seen these problems before. [There were] a few problems [that] we never introduced in class. (p. 51)

You [the instructor] went through materials fast in lecture, and people answered [questions] quickly [so] I didn't follow. (p. 51)

Do these reasons look familiar to you? These students thought their poor performance was the professor's fault, their classmates' fault, or their brain's fault. Now take a look at some student observations about performance in the course after learning about metacognition and metacognitive learning strategies. Again, these responses are taken from Zhao and colleagues (2014).

I have continued to look at the effective learning strategies you introduced to the class last week. I have been going to group tutoring sessions (offered from the learning center on campus) and they helped tremendously. (p. 53)

I have taken a new approach to studying by using some of your suggestions and it does seem to be helping. By previewing the chapter before lecture and studying the notes online, I better understand the material as you go over it. (p. 53)

Thank you for setting aside our class time for this, because I feel that it was really informative and helpful. I identified a few problems with my own study methods, and have since made some changes as you suggested. (p. 53)

Do you see the difference in these responses? The language now focuses on actions the students themselves are taking to improve their performance. Learning about metacognition has helped them to stop seeing themselves as victims and to take responsibility.

Bloom's Taxonomy as an Introduction to Metacognition

So what's the best way to learn about metacognition? Bloom's Taxonomy is an extremely efficient and effective way to help you take metacognitive control of your own learning. Chapter 4 presents a particular method for introducing Bloom's Taxonomy that I have been developing and refining since 2001. I hope it will blow your mind.

Questions to Ask Yourself

1. Describe metacognition in your own words.
2. Do you believe that an early failing grade means a student is not capable of making an A in a course? Why or why not?
3. What lessons did you take away from the Count the Vowels exercise?

Note

1. "'Metacognition' refers to one's knowledge concerning one's own cognitive processes and products or anything related to them, e.g., the learning-relevant properties of information or data" (Flavell, 1976, p. 232).

4

THE POWER OF BLOOM'S TAXONOMY AND THE STUDY CYCLE

"I had never heard of Bloom's Taxonomy and now that you have introduced me to it, I can see that I have been operating in the lower levels of the hierarchy and wondering why I've been struggling! . . . Reflecting upon where in the hierarchy I have been operating, I now understand that there are higher levels and ways of learning, and it motivated me SO MUCH to ascend the levels of higher and deeper learning!"

—David H., third-year student at Westmont College, Santa Barbara, California, personal communication, December 21, 2016

In this chapter, we unleash the power of Bloom's Taxonomy, often shortened to just Bloom's. Bloom's is a hierarchy of learning levels[1] that ascends from very shallow to very deep learning, from rote memorization to the highest levels of understanding and application. We will walk through a four-step formula for learning and absorbing Bloom's. Then we will discuss how to reach higher levels of learning using the study cycle and intense study sessions.

Learning Bloom's Taxonomy: A Four-Step Winning Formula

When I teach Bloom's Taxonomy to students, either in an individual consultation or to a group, I follow a four-step procedure that I have

Figure 4.1. Learning Bloom's Taxonomy: A Four-Step Process

---

1. What's the difference between studying and learning?

2. Would you study harder to make an A on a test or teach the material to the class?

3. Bloom's Taxonomy
Read about each level of the hierarchy and then apply Bloom's to an example like Goldilocks and the Three Bears (see p. 32).

4. At what level of Bloom's have you *been* operating? At what level do you *need* to be operating now?

---

been developing and refining since 2001 (see Figure 4.1). I find that this process leads students through several epiphanies, which leave them optimally motivated to use key learning strategies (see chapter 5) when they leave my presence.

Steps one and two involve reflection questions. First I ask, "What is the difference between studying and learning?" and then I ask, "For which task would you work harder: to make an A on a test or to teach the material to the class?" Step three is a presentation and explanation of Bloom's, whereas step four asks students to assess where they currently are in the hierarchy and where they need to be.

Studying Versus Learning

I begin the process outlined in Figure 4.1 by asking students to articulate the difference between studying and learning. Take a minute to think of your own answer and write it in the space provided.

What is the difference between studying and learning?

Here are some answers I've heard over the years:

- Studying is memorizing information for the exam; learning is when I understand it and can apply it.
- Studying is short term; learning is long term.
- Studying is like being force-fed a plate of gruel; learning is like being set in front of a gourmet table where you get to choose the delicacies you want to eat.
- Studying is what I do the night before the test to make an A; learning is what I do if I know I'm going to have to use that material later on. (My dear colleague from LSU, Pam Ball, often jokes to students, "That way of studying is like renting the information for the test and falling behind on your payments. Right after the test, the information is repossessed!" [personal communication, October 23, 2001])

A first-year dental school student described the difference this way: "Studying is focusing on the 'whats,' but learning is focusing on the 'hows,' 'whys,' and 'what ifs.'" I am particularly fond of this last response. The student who gave it went on to elaborate, "I find that when I focus on the 'whats,' if I forget them I can't re-create the information. But when I focus on the 'hows,' 'whys,' and 'what ifs,' even if I forget the 'whats,' I can re-create them."

I often hear from high school students, "Studying is when I go over what I've already learned." The first time I encountered this idea, I couldn't make sense of it. So I asked, "When did you learn what you are going to study?" The students responded, "In class." It took a few seconds, but then the lightbulb went on. I realized for the first time that some students believe they are actually *learning* information in class and only need to "go over it" in order to do well on exams. Suddenly I understood why so many students wait until the night or two before the test to begin studying. They genuinely believe they have already learned the material in class! Steps three and four will lead those students to a more accurate understanding of the learning process.

After hearing students articulate the difference between studying and learning, I ask them, "Up to this point, have you been operating more in *study* mode or in *learn* mode?" Take a minute now to decide which mode you have been in, and circle one of the two options provided. Then look at the next page to see how most other students have responded.

STUDY MODE   LEARN MODE

The practically unanimous response to this reflection is "study mode." In fact, before I pose the question, most students don't realize there is another mode available. I explain that they are not alone, that most students begin in "study mode," and that I'm going to show them how to switch to "learn mode" and stay there.

Learning It Well Enough to Teach It

Now that we've discussed the difference between studying and learning, I have a second question for you. For which of the following tasks would you work harder: to make an A on a test or to teach the material to the class? Take a second right now and choose one of the options provided. Then see the following page to find out how most students answer.

I WOULD WORK HARDER TO MAKE AN A ON A TEST

I WOULD WORK HARDER TO TEACH THE TEST MATERIAL TO MY CLASS

Although some students do choose the first option, most choose the second. When I ask them why they would work harder to teach the material, they say:

> Well, I have to really know it if I have to teach it!

> If I'm going to teach it, I have to think of questions I might be asked and make sure I can answer them. I don't want to look stupid in front of the class.

> I want to make sure everybody understands and is prepared for the test, so I need to figure out how to explain the information in more than one way.

Here's a fourth question: Until now, have you been in *make-an-A* mode or in *teach-the-material* mode? As before, choose the answer that best applies to you. Then look at the following page to find out how you compare with your fellow students.

MAKE-AN-A MODE   TEACH-THE-MATERIAL MODE

You might not be surprised to learn that virtually everyone admits to being in the first mode. But guess what? You don't need to be an instructor or have your own class to be in "teach-the-material" mode. If you have empty chairs in your room, or stuffed animals, or a coat rack, that's all you need. You can also work with friends or teach the material to family members or pets.

Let's talk about why explaining the information to someone else (real or imagined) works so well. Have you ever found yourself explaining something you thought you totally understood only to discover, in the midst of your explanation, that you were still confused about some part of it? If you hadn't been explaining the information to someone else, then when do you think you would have realized you didn't completely understand the material? When I pose this question to groups of students, they usually respond, in unison, "On the test!" Immediately they see that they need to get out of "make-an-A" mode and into "teach-the-material" mode. In fact, this difference forms the basis of one of the most important learning strategies presented in chapter 5.

Students also report that preparing to teach the material works so well as a learning strategy because they anticipate the *questions* they might be asked. In other words, students aiming to teach the material automatically consider a topic from multiple perspectives because they are actively searching for any confusion that might arise for their "students" instead of reacting to only the biggest, most urgent gaps in their own understanding.

Now that we've completed steps one and two, we are ready to undertake step three, an examination of Bloom's Taxonomy.

Bloom's Taxonomy, Up Close and Personal

Figure 4.2 shows two versions of Bloom's: the original version (Bloom, Englehart, Furst, Hill, & Krathwohl, 1956) and an updated version created by one of the original authors, David Krathwohl, and one of Bloom's students, Lorin Anderson (Anderson et al., 2001).

The original hierarchy of levels (Figure 4.2, left image) ascends from rote memorization (Knowledge) to Comprehension, Application, Analysis, Synthesis, and finally Evaluation. In the revised hierarchy (Figure 4.2,

Figure 4.2. Two Versions of Bloom's Taxonomy: Original and Revised

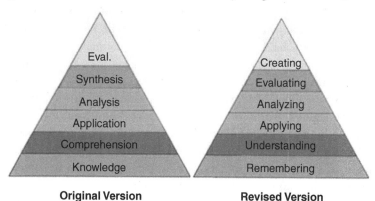

Original Version   **Revised Version**

Note. Figure 4.2 shows two versions of Bloom's Taxonomy: the original version published by Benjamin Bloom and colleagues (1956) and the revised version by a team of his graduate students and their colleagues (Anderson et al., 2001). Adapted with permission from "Bloom's Taxonomy," by R. Overbaugh and L. Schultz, n.d. Retrieved from www.odu.edu/educ/roverbau/Bloom/blooms_taxonomy.htm

right image), the names of the levels have been changed to appear more active and process oriented. Moreover, the top two levels have been reversed. The new taxonomy proceeds from Remembering to Understanding, Applying, Analyzing, Evaluating, and ultimately Creating.

It makes absolutely no difference which form of Bloom's you use, as long as you understand that there are differences between memorizing information, understanding something well enough to put it in your own words, and applying it so that you can answer questions you've never seen before. Bloom's is helpful for students at any level. In fact, after learning about Bloom's, most of my students say, "I wish I had known about Bloom's in high school."

Bloom's in Layman's Terms

Using the new hierarchy, I often explain the six levels as follows: If you're at Remembering, then you have memorized verbatim definitions or formulas, and you could not put that information into your own words. If you're at Understanding, then you can paraphrase the material. You could explain it to your 7-year-old nephew or your 70-year-old grand-mother by creating analogies and examples that apply to their lives. If you're at Applying, then you could use the information you've learned to solve problems you've never seen before. If you're at Analyzing, you can take any concept you've learned and break it down into its component concepts. So if I asked you to give me a minilecture on empirical formulas, you could talk to me about the historical origins of empirical formulas, how to calculate them from percent composition data or CO_2 data, and how they differ from molecular formulas. If you're at Evaluating, you can look at two different processes—proposed by others—and determine which is likelier to be correct, efficient, or desirable. If you're at Creating, you could come up with your own ideas about solving different kinds of problems or designing different processes to accomplish the same goal.

Figure 4.3 shows the revised taxonomy with definitions for each level.

Figure 4.3. Bloom's Taxonomy

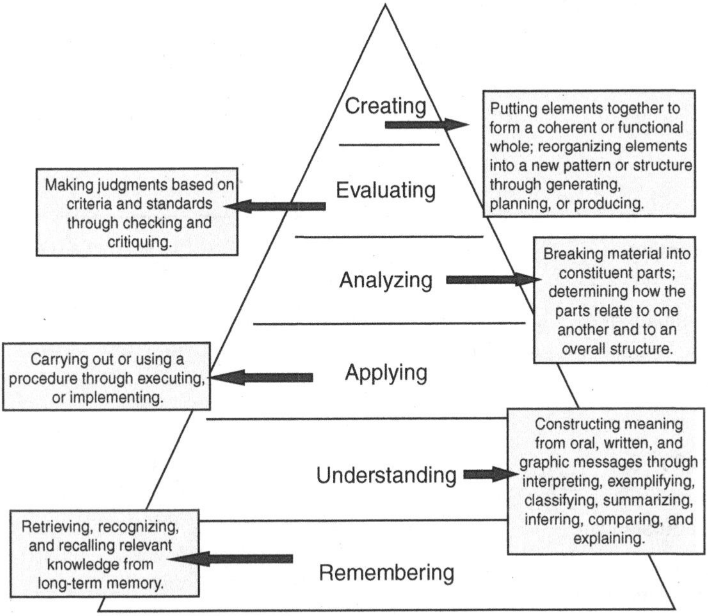

Note. This version of the revised Bloom's Taxonomy features definitions for each level. Adapted from "Image of Revised Versions of Bloom's Taxonomy Featuring Definitions," by R. Overbaugh, n.d. Definitions in boxes are taken from Anderson and colleagues (2001).

More Bloom's: "Goldilocks and the Three Bears"

Let's see how we can apply Bloom's to a familiar childhood story, "Goldilocks and the Three Bears" (see Figure 4.4). You could say that you have mastered Remembering if you can recall all of the things that Goldilocks used at the bears' home. If you can give the reason that Goldilocks preferred Baby Bear's chair, bed, or porridge, then you have mastered Understanding. Next, if you can reasonably predict what items Goldilocks would use when visiting another home, then you have reached the level of Applying. You have mastered Analyzing if you can think critically about the context of the story and call into question particular assumptions; for example, is it plausible that bears could eat porridge out of bowls? You have mastered Evaluating if you can generate reasons that Goldilocks's behavior might be considered justifiable by some and unconscionable by others. Finally, you have scaled the entire hierarchy and mastered Creating

Figure 4.4. Bloom's Taxonomy and Goldilocks

Example

~ Bloom's Levels of Learning~

Applied to "Goldilocks and the Three Bears"

Creating	Write a story about "Goldilocks and the Three Fish". How would it differ from "Goldilocks and the Three Bears"?
Evaluating	Judge whether Goldilocks was good or bad. Defend your opinion.
Analyzing	Compare this story to reality. What events could not really happen?
Applying	Demonstrate what Goldilocks would use if she came to your house.
Understanding	Explain why Goldilocks liked Baby Bear's chair the best.
Remembering	List the items used by Goldilocks while she was in the Bears' house.

Note. Figure 4.4 applies Bloom's Taxonomy to "Goldilocks and the Three Bears" in a way that may be helpful for students. Adapted from *Practicing College Learning Strategies,* 6th ed., by C. Hopper, 2013.

if you can write your own story starring a character named Goldilocks but featuring very different themes and values—perhaps "Goldilocks and the Three Professors."

When you have a solid understanding of Bloom's, you can become an engaged, active learner.

Leveling Up

Now answer the following questions by circling one of the levels of Bloom's, and then turn the page to see how your answers compare to other students'.

Up to this point in your academic life, at what level of Bloom's have you been operating?

REMEMBERING UNDERSTANDING APPLYING
ANALYZING EVALUATING CREATING

What level of Bloom's do you think you need to reach in order to make As in the classes you're currently taking?

REMEMBERING UNDERSTANDING APPLYING
ANALYZING EVALUATING CREATING

Most of your peers say that they have done very well in school at only the first or second level of Bloom's, Remembering or Understanding. But they recognize that in order to meet more intense academic challenges, they need to ascend to level four or above, Analyzing, Evaluating, or Creating.

Figure 4.5 depicts this phenomenon with two bar charts. In 2013, I taught learning strategies to a group of 250 general chemistry students, and after explaining Bloom's, I asked them the two questions on the previous page. Figure 4.5 shows the distribution of their answers. You can see that these two simple questions open students' eyes to what is required of them.

Figure 4.5. Bloom's Taxonomy in High School and College

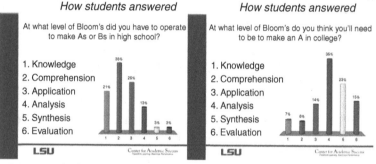

Note. Figure 4.5 demonstrates that, after learning about Bloom's Taxonomy, most students recognize that college courses will require them to operate at a higher level of learning than high school classes do. The categories are based on the original version of Bloom's Taxonomy (Bloom et al., 1956).

Ascending the Levels of Bloom's Taxonomy:
Use the Study Cycle With Intense Study Sessions

Okay, so how do students go about pursuing deep learning goals and ascending the levels of Bloom's? They use the metacognitive strategies presented in chapter 5, all under the umbrella of the study cycle (Figure 4.6). The study cycle consists of five steps:

1. Preview
2. Attend class
3. Review
4. Do intense study sessions
5. Assess

Figure 4.6. The Study Cycle

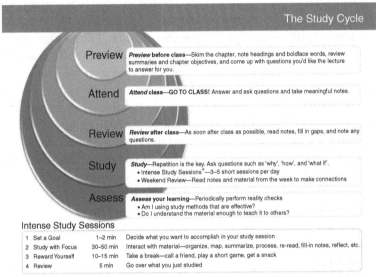

Note. Figure 4.6 presents the study cycle given to students at LSU's CAS. The cycle is based on F. L. Christ's (1997) Learning Cycle. © 2010 Louisiana State University, Center for Academic Success. Used with permission. This work is reproduced and distributed with the permission of Louisiana State University. No other use is permitted without the express prior written permission of Louisiana State University. Contact cas@lsu.edu for permission.

The first step, preview reading, lays the foundation for what you will encounter in class. By previewing, you're making sure that your brain sees the big picture and understands how the concepts you're about to learn fit together. Previewing will be more fully explained in chapter 5. The next step in the cycle is to go to class. Even though missing class may not have been a big deal in high school and though your professors may post lecture notes online, it is imperative that you go to class in college. College lectures are very different from high school classes, and a plethora of information will be presented in class that will not appear in the condensed, distilled lecture notes. Moreover, class time represents a golden opportunity to ask crucial questions. Only by attending class will you be able to keep up with your courses.

Here it may be worth noting that some professors have decided that instead of lecturing, they prefer a more active classroom requiring frequent student participation. These professors want to give their students the opportunity to *discover* and *experience* the ideas and concepts presented in class. If you have a professor like this, I encourage you to cherish the opportunity you have to use class time for active, lasting learning. Some students instead resent their professors for "not teaching them" or, worse, for distracting them from other things they had planned to do during class. But these students fail to see that their professor is actually saving them time by allowing them to engage in metacognition and immediately start ascending levels of Bloom's. However, if you are a student who prefers a lecture format because that's how you feel you learn best, try to jump in and take the opportunity to see what it's like to learn on the fly with others, something you may need to do at some point in your professional life.

As soon as possible after class, you should undertake step three and review your notes, recalling what happened in class and explaining it to yourself, thereby enhancing the memory of what happened in class (Medina, 2008). Have you ever seen a movie more than once? Did you notice that the second time you saw it, you noticed things that you didn't even know were there the first time? Reviewing is like watching the movie the second time. Your brain will see things that it didn't before. As you review, actively recall the instructor's voice, address any gaps in your notes, elaborate on details you had no time to write down during the lecture, and take note of any issues that need clarifying. If you want to know more about the cognitive science of memory and learning, *Brain Rules* (Medina, 2008) and *Make It Stick* (Brown, Roediger, & McDaniel, 2014) are great places to start.

Previewing and reviewing are powerful and efficient ways to support learning. Some students just get to class 10 minutes early and do their previewing immediately before the lecture. And if there's no class following the lecture, they just review for 10 minutes after lecture. Lickety-split.

During the fourth step in the cycle, students use the framework of intense study sessions (see bottom of Figure 4.6). These sessions are effective because they enable students to break their work down into manageable chunks. Intense study sessions can be as short as 15 to 20 minutes (appropriate for students with attention-deficit/hyperactivity disorder) or as long as 75 to 90 minutes, though 50 to 60 minutes is a typical duration. An intense study session has four parts:

1. Set specific goals.
2. Do active learning tasks.
3. Take a break/have a reward.
4. Review.

Use the first few minutes of an intense study session to set a manageable number of achievable goals. Then engage in learning activities that have been proven to work, activities we will thoroughly explore in the next chapter. After doing the heavy lifting for 30 to 50 minutes, but not longer than a period for which you can maintain good focus, take a 10- to 15-minute break. The break is crucial for restoring energy and motivation, and for allowing the information you've just absorbed time to "sink in." In fact, Doyle and Zakrajsek (2013) encourage students to "engage in periods of wakeful rest, including daydreaming and thinking, following new learning" (p. 24), citing research from Dewar, Alber, Butler, Cowan, and Della Sala (2012) that suggests rest following learning is crucial for memory formation. Doyle and Zakrajsek also suggest napping for 20 to 30 minutes as an effective way to consolidate memories. Wouldn't you know it, a short nap fits right in with step 3 of a 60- to 90-minute study cycle. Whether you take your break asleep or awake, when you come back refreshed, take 5 minutes to review what you've just studied. During this final step in the study cycle, after intense study sessions, assess how well you have learned the material you studied by engaging in self-evaluation. Determine whether you need to tweak your learning strategies and adjust them accordingly. For example, perhaps flashcards did not quite do the trick, so you might decide to try concept mapping in subsequent intense study sessions.

If you do two or three sessions during the day between classes, and another couple of sessions at night, you will have studied 4 to 5 hours that day without breaking a sweat. In fact, when asked to specify what changes he'd made to turn around his academic performance, one student said, "I use that Power Hour thing." (Intense study session. Power Hour. Tomato, tomahto.)

I want to reiterate that short, intense study sessions, even as short as 10 minutes, are great for students who cannot imagine sitting down to study for an entire hour. During a 10-minute session, set goals in the first minute, work for 8 minutes, and take a minute to review. I know of students who do 10 to 20 of these short sessions per day, at a relaxed pace throughout the day, with great success.

Drum Roll, Please: 10 Metacognitive Strategies

In the next chapter, we will discuss specific active learning tasks that you can use to ace your courses.

Questions to Ask Yourself

1. What is the study cycle and what is it used for?
2. List the steps of the study cycle and why each step is important.
3. What is an intense study session and what is it used for?
4. What duration for an intense study session do you think might work best for you? Why?
5. List all of the courses or classes you are taking now, and next to each, write down the level of Bloom's you think you need to reach in order to do well in that particular course or class.

Note

1. Many people have expressed to me that they do not think of Bloom's Taxonomy as a hierarchy and believe it is a mistake to represent it as a pyramid. They argue that levels do not proceed in order and instead are constantly

intertwining. As support for their argument, they note that a student can create something without knowing basic foundational information. I do think that faction has a valid point. However, I like presenting Bloom's to students in hierarchy form because I want them to understand that they will likely not be able to *apply* concepts that they do not *understand* if they have not *memorized* particular facts. I like to illustrate this point with a story. Our older daughter is a professor in the allergy and immunology section of the department of pediatrics at Baylor College of Medicine. When she joined the faculty, her responsibilities included accompanying the residents on their rounds. One day, she asked a resident if it is advisable to prescribe pseudoepinephrine-based drugs like Sudafed or Actifed to pregnant women. She expected him to think critically about her question and answer accordingly. Instead, he whipped out his smartphone and looked it up in the *Physicians' Desk Reference*. He correctly answered, "No," but when she asked him why, he had no clue. She explained to the residents that drugs that constrict blood vessels are never a good idea for pregnant women. My point is that many students nowadays think that they do not need to know anything because they can just look up everything on the Internet. I try to help them see that no one can solve problems using information he or she has only just read. We can solve problems and do critical thinking only with information already stored in our brains. The pyramidal form of Bloom's handily makes this point.

5

METACOGNITIVE LEARNING STRATEGIES AT WORK

"Well, it's official. Doing my homework problems as if they were quiz questions, after studying my notes and practicing teaching the material works really well for me. Just wanted to share with you my grade on the second Chem 1421 exam: 95, A!"

—Sydnie L., first-year honors chemistry student at LSU,
personal communication, October 17, 2013

In this chapter, I lay out the top 10 learning strategies that make possible the dramatic results you've heard about so far.

Ten Strategies to Optimize Your Academic Performance

The rest of this chapter lists and elucidates 10 metacognitive strategies, the first three of which are powerful reading strategies I have found particularly useful to teach my students:

1. Previewing
2. Preparing for active reading
3. Paraphrasing

4. Reading actively
5. Using the textbook even if it is not required
6. Going to class and taking notes by hand
7. Doing homework *without* using solved examples as a guide
8. Teaching material to a real or imagined audience
9. Working in pairs or groups
10. Creating practice exams

Keep in mind that you do not have to implement all of these strategies to see improvement in your grades or enjoy deeper understanding of the subjects you are studying. You can pick and choose what works for you, though there are some strategies that are so effective—namely, the reading and homework strategies—that everyone should use them. Finally, I want to acknowledge that you may already be using powerful and effective strategies other than the 10 presented here.

My Introduction to the Reading Strategies

Remember Travis, the psychology student who flunked his first two tests (Figure 3.1)? During my first conversation with Travis, I asked him what he thought his problem was. He began to tell me about all of the reading assignments he was responsible for completing. He told me, "I do the reading, but when I get to the test I don't really remember it. I know that I've read it, but I don't remember it when it counts, so I know I'm not really getting a lot out of my reading."

Long before I met with Travis, I had heard that same refrain from so very many students: undergraduates, graduate students, business, law, medical students, you name it. I didn't really know what to tell these students. I might have given vague advice like, "Slow down when you're reading," or "Answer the questions in the text." So in 2005, when I learned about a four-week workshop on reading strategies given by the Institute of Reading Development, I decided to see if I could learn some strategies to help my students.

Incidentally, because the institute runs this workshop all over the country, my first-grade grandson was attending that same workshop in his hometown! I often joke that when I first learned that there were graduate degrees in "college reading," I thought it was an oxymoron because I just *knew* that I had learned to read in first grade. But what I learned in that workshop I definitely had not been taught in first grade or any grade after that. These strategies turned Travis's performance around (Figure 3.1), and they can do the same for you.

What's So Hard About Reading?

What happens when you read? Well, if you're like most people, you begin reading and all is well until your mind starts to wander. But your brain doesn't immediately realize that it is no longer paying attention because your eyes are still tracking the text. Plus, if you're a subvocalizer, like I am, you can hear the words as you read, even though you're thinking about something entirely unrelated. It's not until you get farther down the page that you realize, "Oh, I stopped paying attention ages ago and have no idea what I'm reading."

At this point, what do you usually do? If you're like most people, you go back and reread the text from the beginning, but this time around, you concentrate harder to keep yourself from running off the rails. And you will probably get a little farther, but only a little, before the same thing happens again. And then what do you do? Start over. Again. You can see where this is going.

But you can prevent this vicious cycle by engaging in particular practices before you start to read. The following three reading strategies should be used in concert for the biggest impact. Think of them as one big active reading strategy with three steps.

Active Reading, Step One: Previewing

For maximally engaged reading, you must give yourself a preview of what you're about to read (**strategy #1**). We know the brain is much more efficient at learning when it has a big picture and then acquires individual details to fill in that big picture (e.g., Klingner & Vaughn, 1999). How do you give it that big picture? Look at the section headings, bold print, italicized words, and any charts or graphs in the portion of reading you have chosen. If you are reading a novel, then read the first line of every paragraph.

To experience the power of previewing, let's do an exercise (Bransford, 1979). You're going to read the short passage that follows, and I'm going to ask you three questions about it. You can jot your answers down in the space provided. The first question will be, "What specific task is this passage about?" and the second and third questions will be asked after you've finished the reading.

> The procedure is actually quite simple. First you arrange things into different groups. Of course one pile may be sufficient depending on how much there is to do. If you have to go somewhere else due to lack of facilities that is the next step; otherwise, you are pretty well set. It is important not to overdo things. That is, it is better to do too few things at once than too many. In the short run this may not seem important but complications can easily arise. A mistake can be expensive as well. At first, the whole procedure will seem complicated. Soon, however, it will become just another facet of life. It is difficult to foresee any end to the necessity for this task in the immediate future, but, then, one can never tell. After the procedure is completed, one arranges the materials into different groups again. Then they can be put into their appropriate places. Eventually they will be used once more, and the whole cycle will then have to be repeated. However, that is a part of life. (pp. 134–135)

What specific task is this passage about?

Where can you go if you lack the facilities?

How can a mistake be expensive?

Give yourself a minute to think about it before moving on.

If you are stumped, you're not alone. I have never heard a correct answer to the first question during an individual consultation, and in my student and faculty workshops, occasionally 2 or 3 people out of 50 figure out the answer.

Now I will reveal to you that this passage is about doing laundry. Reread the passage and try to answer the questions, now that you have an idea of the subject matter.

Did the passage sound different to you? Were you able to engage with it more actively and derive much more meaning from its sentences? Do the questions now seem trivial rather than mystifying?

Knowing that the passage is about laundry is the equivalent of previewing and seeing "Laundry" as a bold heading. If you have some idea of what you are about to read, your brain can recognize and process much more information than if you just dive headlong into your reading.

Have you ever had the experience that you go to class and the information is going from the PowerPoint slides onto your notes without passing through your brain? That is a wasted hour. But I want you to make every hour count. If you've done the previewing, you have the skeleton you need so that during lecture you can put all the necessary meat on those bones. I have been gratified to hear in many conversations with individual students, "Wow, lecture makes so much more sense when I preview."

Active Reading, Step Two: Previewing on Steroids.
Come Up With Questions the Reading Can Answer

Once you've looked at the bold and italicized text as well as charts and graphs, you still need to do one more thing before you begin to read. You need to give yourself a *reason* to read. Just like no four-year-old likes hearing, "You have to," neither does your brain. So you need to come up with questions that you want the reading to answer for you (**strategy #2**). Then you've tapped into your genuine curiosity and are much more motivated to read.

Let's say I'm reading a chapter in a general chemistry textbook about acids and bases. The terms *strong acid* and *weak acid* would probably be in a distinctive font. My question might be, "What is the difference between strong acids and weak acids?" So now I've given myself motivation to read the text.

Or if I were going to read a chapter on buffer solutions, I might see "weak acids" in bold or italicized print. I might ask myself, "What do weak acids have to do with buffers? Are they different from strong acids?" When I start to read, my mind will be looking for the answers, and I will be able to stay focused longer.

Active Reading, Step Three: Paraphrasing the Correct Way

Now that you've previewed the text, and you've generated interesting questions that you hope the text will answer, you're ready to begin reading. Here is the crucial instruction: When you start, read only one paragraph at a time. Just read the first paragraph. Stop. Put the information in that first paragraph in your own words.

Now move on to the second paragraph and do the same thing, except this time when you paraphrase, fold in the information that was in the first paragraph. After you read the third paragraph, your paraphrase should contain all of the information from the beginning of the passage—and so on and so forth, ad infinitum (**strategy #3**). This way, you break a big task down into manageable chunks, yet the information from the chunks is integrated into a complete understanding of the topic at hand.

Does that process sound like it will take a very long time? Guess what? Every single one of my students who has discussed with me their use of this method reports that it takes less time to finish their reading assignments with this system than with the one they had been using. Graduate students in particular tell me that it helps them move briskly through research papers. When I ask my students, "Why do you think it works?" they say, "I'm not rereading or having a bunch of false starts." So although they are reading more slowly, they are only moving *forward*, so the end comes much more quickly and with much deeper understanding. The tortoise and the hare. Slow and steady wins the race.

Flashcards and Maps and Outlines, Oh My!

The previous three reading strategies should often be supplemented by activities like highlighting; taking notes; jotting down questions; and creating flashcards, concept or mind maps, and outlines (**strategy #4**). These tasks can be undertaken while reading the textbook, supplemental reading, or class notes. Appendix F provides descriptions of some of the most common and popular study tools used by students today.

I was surprised to learn from speaking with groups of students over the years that even as students are actively reading their textbooks many of them skip over example problems or assessment questions that appear in the text. However, it's important to always do these kinds of problems and questions in order to maximize one's comprehension.

Joshua, an engineering major who took general chemistry in his freshman year, learned to love active reading. This student came to me with a D average in general chemistry because he had scored 68, 50, and 50 on the first three tests. After working with me, he scored 87 on both of the next two tests and cranked out a 97 on the final exam. Joshua earned an A in the course and a 3.8 GPA that semester. When I asked him via e-mail which strategies worked for him, he responded, "I think what I did different was make sidenotes in each chapter, and as I progressed into the next chapter I was able to refer to these notes. I would say that in chemistry, everything builds from the previous topic." Indeed.

Textbooks, Please

We interrupt our regularly scheduled programming for a public service announcement. Please, please, please do whatever you need to do to make sure you have access to your course textbooks. I hear horror stories every week about students who did not have access to books in high school, or if they did, they couldn't take the books home. Many students have even told me that their professors have given explicit, blanket permission not to buy the book. These professors tell their students that everything they need to know is in their notes.

Let's do a brief exercise. Look at Figure 5.1 and tell me the first word that comes to mind.

Figure 5.1. Fill-in-the-Blank Exercise

C_T

Did you see the word *cat*? Or perhaps *cot* or *cut*? If you know something very well, then large chunks of it can be missing or misordered, and you can still recognize it. This fact is the basis of some of your ingenious texting abbreviations or clever personalized license plates.

But what if our culture had no cats, cots, or cuts? Or what if we used different words to describe those things? Then you would look at Figure 5.1 and it would mean nothing to you. *That is the experience of students who try to use lecture notes to learn complex subjects.* The notes are the C_T version of the information. That's why the textbook has so many more pages than the lecture notes. It has charts! It has graphs! Diagrams! Supplemental problems! It's there to help you (**strategy #5**). When your instructors read the lecture notes, their minds fill in everything that is missing, but your mind cannot yet fill in those gaps. You need the textbook.

Have you ever encountered an exam that covered material you didn't remember learning in class? But your instructor swore up and down that he or she distinctly remembered covering it? The phenomenon just described explains how you and your instructor are both correct. That material was in the notes, slides, or board work that your instructor saw but not in what you saw. You saw C_T, but your instructor thought he or she had presented CAT.

When I am trying to convince students to buy textbooks, I explain to them that their instructors' brains have all of the missing information to flesh out the lecture notes. Then I ask them, "But does your brain have all the information in organic chemistry or cell biology or philosophy or multivariable calculus to fill in the gaps?" They shake their heads no. I go on to ask, "When the professor writes the test, is he or she writing it based on what his or her brain sees in the notes or what your brain sees in the notes?" They quickly see my point.

To those who protest that textbooks are expensive, I ask, "What's more expensive, the textbook or not getting into medical school because you made a C in chemistry?" Most find the money for the textbook. To the holdouts I say, "Okay, buy the book and use it for a couple of weeks. If it isn't useful, return it to the bookstore for whatever they will give you, come back and see me, and I will write you a personal check for the difference." I have never, ever had to write a check. Every single student has come back and said something to the effect of, "Wow! I can't believe what a big difference the book makes! I had no idea it would be so helpful."

But please do not think I'm unsympathetic to the plight of cash-strapped students needing to shell out hundreds or thousands of dollars for books twice a year. There are several options for students who understand the importance of textbooks but who have no desire to pay full price for one:

- Use the textbook copies made available through your campus library or learning center.
- Take advantage of interlibrary loan. Your campus librarian can show you how.
- Borrow the textbook from a student who has previously taken the course.
- Rent your textbook online from a student who has just finished the course or through a service provided by your academic institution.
- Buy used textbooks online or from students who have recently finished the course.
- Get permission from the instructor to use an earlier, cheaper edition of the textbook.
- E-mail or call the textbook publishing company to see if they offer e-book rental for the duration of the semester.
- See if your student government has a textbook loan program whereby they collect or purchase textbooks and then loan them out for the semester. If there is no such program, ask your student government to sponsor one or take the initiative and start one yourself.

Remember to always get recommendations for used textbook vendors or rental services from your instructor, fellow students, academic advisers, or campus learning center staff in order to avoid getting scammed.

The bottom line is that if you do not have your course textbooks, the four effective metacognitive strategies just presented are impossible for you to use. During my initial session with Joshua, I asked him if he had the textbook. He replied, "There is no textbook for the course." Then I asked him to show me his syllabus. Sure enough, the textbook was listed as "optional." Because it was optional, Joshua had not even seen it on the syllabus. (Chapter 7 contains indispensable information about how to get the most out of a syllabus.) I convinced Joshua to buy the textbook, and the rest is history. Without textbooks, neither Joshua nor Dana nor a host of other students would have soared in their classes or fulfilled their larger goals.

I implore you to buy and use the textbooks for all of your courses.

How to Use a Textbook

Permit me another story, if not an explicit strategy, if you would. About 10 years ago, I was working in the tutorial center at the LSU CAS, and a young woman arrived and said she was having problems arranging substances in order of increasing entropy. So I said, "Okay. Tell me what entropy is." She replied, "I don't know what it is." She had had the foresight to bring her book to the center, and it was sitting on the desk in front of her. So I said, "What if I told you that I would make you give me all of your tickets to the LSU football games left in the season if you do not give me a definition of *entropy* in the next five minutes. What would you do?" She said, "Well, I guess I'd just have to miss all the rest of the games."

"Noooo, no, no, no, no, you don't have to miss the rest of the games. In fact, there's something in this room that would keep you from having to give up all your tickets."

She looked around the room, scanned everything on each of the four walls, and then finally looked down at the table. It hit her:

"The book?"
"Yes!!! The book!"
"But I don't know what chapter it's in."
"How could you find out what chapter it's in?"

I tell this story to let you know that if you do not know how to use a textbook because you have never had to use one, you are not alone. Many students arrive on college campuses never having used a table of contents or an index. If you are one of them, just be aware that the table of contents is at the front of the book and lays out the content and location of all of the subjects covered in the book. The index is at the back of the book and contains an alphabetized list of terms and where they appear in the book. To look up a general topic, the table of contents is useful, but to find more specific terms or concepts, try the index.

Go to Class and Take Notes by Hand

Many students underestimate the value of going to class and have not learned how to be engaged in class. You should, without a shadow of a doubt, go to every single class and take notes by hand (**strategy #6**). Many students these days take notes on their laptops, tablets, or even smartphones. But recent studies show that taking notes by hand results in more learning than does taking notes with a laptop, partly because students are forced to paraphrase when they take notes by hand (Mueller & Oppenheimer, 2014). If you are afraid you will miss something important, you can record the lecture and listen to it at a later time.

If you have to miss class, get the notes from a reliable student rather than just downloading lecture slides or notes (Hoffmann & McGuire, 2010). A fellow student's notes will have explanations and additional material not present in the lecture notes.

I'll end this section with a few words about *where* to sit in class: If you want to maximize your impact, sit in one of the front rows or choose a seat farther back but near the center (Adams & Biddle, 1970). This area of the classroom or lecture hall is sometimes called "The T Zone" because it is shaped like a T with the top of the T corresponding to the front rows. The advantage of sitting in the T Zone is twofold. First, *you* can easily see the instructor and all of the teaching materials; plus you have a better shot at getting your questions answered as they arise. Second, even if you're silent as a stone, the *instructor* can't help but register you as someone who faithfully and conscientiously comes to class. This small but powerful choice to sit in the T Zone sets you up beautifully to have pleasant and productive discussions with the instructor during office hours. Of course, there's no need to despair if, because of your schedule, you can't ever get to class early enough to catch a spot in the T Zone. Being in class is sufficient, and the instructor doesn't need to recognize you in order to establish good rapport during office hours. But if it is possible to sit in the T Zone, you won't regret it. In addition to the benefits already noted, it can sharpen your focus and help you stay alert and engaged in class (Staley, 2007).

Use Your Homework to Test Your Knowledge

Remember Dana, the undergraduate on the verge of leaving physics who now holds a master's degree in medical physics (chapter 3)? This strategy completely transformed her performance on physics exams. In fact, most of my science students who come to me when they are earning low Cs, Ds, or Fs, and who subsequently begin to make A grades, say that doing homework without using solved examples as a guide (**strategy #7**) is the one change that turned everything around.

When introducing this strategy, I ask students, "If there were a camera recording everything you do when you sit down to do your homework, tell me exactly what it would see."

"Okay, I sit down and I open my book and then I look at the first problem."

"Have you ever looked at a problem and immediately decided to flip back in the textbook to look for an example?"

"Yes, Dr. McGuire! How did you know?"

"Because everybody is doing it. I did it myself when I was in school."

Over the years, I have learned that most students do their homework by looking at example problems in the textbook or in their class notes and trying to copy the steps laid out there in order to arrive at the correct answer. *This method is exactly the wrong way to go about doing homework problems.*

Homework and example problems in the textbook and class notes should always be treated as an opportunity to test yourself. Study for the homework the way you would study for a quiz. Before looking at the homework questions or problems, actively read the relevant part of the textbook or any class notes. As you encounter example problems, work those problems *without referring to the given solutions.* For each problem, even if you get stuck and don't know the next step, do your very best to power through and arrive at an answer. Then *check only the final answer* and not the steps taken to work out the solution. If your answer is incorrect, then reread the text or class notes to investigate why and where you made mistakes. Much important and deep learning takes place during that investigation process. When you arrive at the correct answer, compare your *approach* to that of the textbook or instructor. If the approaches are different, ask yourself whether both approaches are valid. Why or why not? If they are both valid, do you prefer your approach or the alternative approach? Why? This process provides many opportunities for reflection, metacognition, and deep learning. Additionally, sometimes someone else's method just doesn't immediately "click" with your brain. If you look at that method before trying your own, you may become locked into that way of thinking about the problem, which will be an unnecessary burden you carry throughout the rest of the course and perhaps beyond. Relying on others' methods restricts your creative flexibility and mental agility.

After working the example problems in this manner, then turn to the homework. Do two or three problems at a time, treating each problem like a quiz or test question, looking at answers or worked-out solutions only after having made your best attempt to solve the group of problems.

If you think you lack the confidence to try this strategy, convinced that if you do not look at complete solutions you will be endlessly staring at a blank page, I suggest you try the following: Spend at least five minutes going through the reading or class notes to see if you can figure out how to begin the problem. If after five minutes you are still stumped, you should look only at the first step of the worked example, and continue solving the problem. If you're still at a loss, spend another five minutes on step two, and continue in this way until you have solved the problem. Using this method, you maximize your opportunity to solve problems independently. I always tell my students, "Practice problems, wherever they come from, are your brain's best resource for demonstrating that it can do all the problems likely to appear on a test without relying on an example as a guide."

Whenever I present this strategy to students, as soon as I explain to them that they should try to figure out where they made a mistake before looking at solutions, I ask them, "At this point in the process, do you think that mistakes are good or bad?" All of the student groups with whom I've worked collectively answer that mistakes are good. Mistakes represent a golden opportunity (Zull, 2011). When I ask students why mistakes are good, they answer:

> You learn from your mistakes.
>
> You can correct your mistakes.
>
> You never make the same mistake twice.
>
> You learn where your mind has a tendency to go wrong.
>
> You won't lose points if you make a mistake now.

Have you ever received a graded exam and thought, "Oh, no! I made so many careless mistakes!"? I believe there is almost no such thing as a careless mistake. Mistakes look careless only in retrospect. These kinds of mistakes *must* be made, sometimes repeatedly. "So," I tell students, "you're either going to make your mistakes now, during the homework process, or . . . where?" "On the test," they correctly answer. I was surprised to find that once students understand the importance of making mistakes during the homework process, they often stop using websites like cramster.com or chegg.com to complete their homework assignments. They understand that by doing homework in the correct way, they are training their brain for the task it will face during the exam: solving problems without any model or guide.

One final note. When you are moving through example problems and homework, or quizzes and tests, you should begin with simple problems and progress to more complex ones that test mastery of more than one concept. We will see in chapter 7 that early success is a powerful motivator, and early failure is a powerful discourager. So you need to give yourself opportunities for success. Often, but not always, homework or exam problems are arranged from easiest to most difficult. If the easiest homework problems are too difficult, you can search for problems in the textbook easier than the homework and start with those. Even assessing the difficulty of problems requires metacognitive activity and helps you absorb the material more deeply.

Using homework as an opportunity to assess learning is an extremely powerful strategy. Alongside the reading strategies, it is one of the most effective and transformative strategies you can use.

Students as Teachers

You can also assess your understanding of material by teaching it to a friend, who may or may not be in the same course, or by pretending to teach it to an empty sofa, a pet, or even your own reflection (**strategy #8**). In trying to explain concepts in a way that others can understand, you become aware of the gaps in your understanding or of details that are not entirely clear to you. You can then try to clear up your confusion on your own or ask a fellow student or instructor. Students usually appreciate the power of this strategy due to our previous discussion about "make-an-A" mode versus "teach-the-material" mode (chapter 4).

Come Together, Right Now

Working in pairs or groups, in addition to working alone, can be a powerful supplement to the other learning strategies (**strategy #9**). In groups, students often have the opportunity to teach (see preceding section) and learn from each other. Working in groups helps students engage in one of the major aspects of metacognition, accurately judging their own learning (Figure 3.2). Cook, Kennedy, and McGuire (2013) assert that students in groups "evaluate each other's thinking [and are] more likely to be metacognitive about how they approach information" (p. 962) than when they work alone. When discussing study groups in student workshops, I sometimes ask, "Why are study groups helpful?" Students respond:

If I say something wrong other people can correct me.

I can hear the way other people think about the material.

Of course, you must actually be working rather than socializing. Vygotsky (1978) and Bruner (1985) have established that in order to be effective, study groups must engage in both discussion and problem-solving activities.[1]

Play Detective: Piece Together a Mock Exam Using Homework and Quizzes as Clues

Have you ever tried to find out what will be on an exam only to find yourself completely stonewalled by your instructor? I have good news for you. From the syllabus, lecture notes, homework assignments, and quizzes, you can deduce the topics and problem types that will appear on the exam. Then you can create an outline of an exam or create your own practice exam using the bank of problems in the textbook and, if applicable, supplemental optional problems provided throughout the unit by the instructor (**strategy #10**). Practice exams can also be made in groups, with each student responsible for a different topic.

There is powerful evidence demonstrating the effectiveness of testing as a way to reinforce, deepen, and enrich learning. In articles for the *New York Times*, science writer Benedict Carey (2010, 2014) shares evidence from Roediger and Karpicke (2006) and Pennebaker, Gosling, and Ferrell (2013) that illustrates the power of testing.

Roediger and Karpicke (2006) asked college students to study science passages in preparation for a later reading comprehension test. If students studied these passages in two sequential sessions, they performed well on a test given right after the study sessions, but the material did not stick. However, another group of students, who studied the passages only once and in the second session took a practice test, did well on an assessment two days later and another test a full week later. Testing is a powerful way to deepen and lengthen learning.

Pennebaker and colleagues (2013) did something radical with their introductory psychology course at the University of Texas. Instead of giving a final exam, they replaced it with "a series of short quizzes that students took on their laptops at the beginning of each class" (Carey, 2014, para. 3). The professors reported that the students groused and grumbled because they had to constantly prepare for these never-ending quizzes. But compared to another set of students taking the same course, these students not only boasted better course grades than their peers but also did better "on a larger quiz that included 17 of the same questions [from both] quizzes and on the other class's midterm" (Carey, 2014, para. 5). Carey (2014) correctly notes that "the quizzes were especially beneficial for the type of students—many from low-performing high schools—who don't realize how far behind they are until it's too late" (para. 5).

Practice testing works. If you want to ace the real exam, you should practice first.

The Strategies: A Recap

These 10 strategies make up the heart of my work and the heart of this book. You don't have to use all 10 strategies to see fast and dramatic results like the ones Travis, Dana, and Joshua enjoyed. I recommend you begin with the reading, classroom, and homework strategies, and add more as you continue on your metacognitive journey.

A Useful Resource

Appendix C contains the Learning Strategies Inventory (LSI), a tool to help you assess the current state of your academic health in a particular course. You indicate which strategies you are currently using via a true/false assessment, and the LSI predicts the grade you will earn in the course. The purpose of the LSI is not to shame you into recognizing what you are doing wrong. Its purpose is to further convince you that your performance directly correlates with your *behavior* rather than any innate fixed ability. In fact, one major purpose of everything I have shared with you is to help you attribute your results only to your actions, to help you change your mindset. In the next chapter, we will discover the power of mindset.

Are You Convinced Yet?

When I present these strategies to a student in an individual consultation, at the end of the session, I usually ask two questions to determine the likelihood that the student will begin using the strategies. I'll ask you those questions right now. On a scale of 1 to 10, how different are the strategies we have talked about from the ones you have been using up to this point? (A response of 1 represents no difference at all; 10 is a difference as extreme as day and night.)

1   2   3   4   5   6   7   8   9   10

On a scale of 1 to 10, how *motivated* are you to start using the strategies? (1 is not at all; 10 is "I can't wait to start them today!")

1   2   3   4   5   6   7   8   9   10

In response to the first question, if you reported a number between 7 and 10, I know that you recognize the difference between what you have been doing and the actions I am encouraging you to take. In response to the second question, if you reported a number between 8 and 10, then I am confident that you will in fact try one or more of the strategies. If your numbers were lower, there's nothing wrong with that, but I would encourage you to look at the strategies again to try to find even more differences between what you've been doing up to this point and what the strategies recommend. For example, someone might look at the reading strategy and think, "Okay, I paraphrase in the margins; I'm doing that," but the strategy is more specific than that. The devil is in the details. That goes for all of the strategies. I would also encourage you to develop a plan, like getting a buddy to hold you accountable for making changes, in order to increase the chances that your understanding will deepen and your grades will improve.

I want to reinforce to you that no matter what your grades are now, your future performance will depend only on whether you use the strategies and not at all on how "smart" you think you are or how "smart" other people think you are. I know with every fiber of my being that all students can be successful.

Activities for You

1. Name at least one strategy you would be interested in trying for a week or two.
2. Take a look at Appendix F and list one or more study tools you think might work for you.

Note

1. I often warn students against the "divide and conquer" strategy that some study groups use, in which each member of the study group is responsible for a portion of the material. The danger is that each member will learn his or her territory very well, but will have a significantly shallower understanding of the majority of the material.

6

WHY YOUR MINDSET
ABOUT INTELLIGENCE
MATTERS

"I'm just not good at chemistry."

—Joshua, an engineering major at LSU who finished a general chemistry
course with an A, personal communication, May 13, 2011

This chapter is based on the work of Carol Dweck (2006), a professor of psychology at Stanford University. Her book *Mindset* has proved so important and the ideas within it have been so useful that they deserve their own chapter.

Fixed Intelligence or Intelligence That Can Grow?

Dweck (2006) found that people commonly hold one of two mindsets about intelligence: They believe intelligence is fixed, or they believe it can grow. Put differently, some people believe that each person is born holding a set of intellectual cards, and little can be done to augment that hand, whereas others believe that they can acquire a few aces through effort and action. You will not be surprised to hear that, although I once had a fixed mindset, the astonishing results I have seen from students have converted me to a growth mindset.

David Shenk (2010) gives several evidence-based arguments to support his assertion that "intelligence is a process, not a thing" (p. 29). But regardless of the truth about intelligence, *beliefs* about intelligence have been repeatedly demonstrated to have an enormous effect on performance.

Mindset as Master of Your Fate

Figure 6.1, adapted from Dweck's (2006) book, contrasts the likely attitudes and actions of a person with a fixed mindset with those of someone who has a growth mindset. As shown, people with a fixed mindset tend to avoid challenges, give up easily, ignore criticism, and find the success of others threatening. By contrast, people with a growth mindset embrace challenges, persevere, use effort to achieve mastery, benefit from criticism, and find motivational fuel in the success of others.

We can conclude from Dweck's work that a fixed mindset is kryptonite in any arena, including school. Yet so many of us believe that intelligence is largely innate and fixed. These beliefs are devastating because our confidence, or lack thereof, that we can successfully perform a task greatly influences how motivated we are to even attempt that task (Ambrose, Bridges, DiPietro, Lovett, & Norman, 2010).

Three Illustrations of the Power of Mindset

Mindset (Dweck, 2006) contains references to a number of peer-reviewed, published research articles supporting the findings summarized in Figure 6.1. Here I present the following illustrations supporting Dweck's findings, chosen somewhat arbitrarily given the treasure trove of supporting research: (a) a study from David H. Uttal (1997) about the attitudes of Asian and American mothers and children about mathematical ability; (b) an intervention cited in a paper from Aguilar, Walton, and Wieman (2014); and (c) anecdotal evidence from a middle school math teacher.

Figure 6.1. Fixed and Growth Mindsets

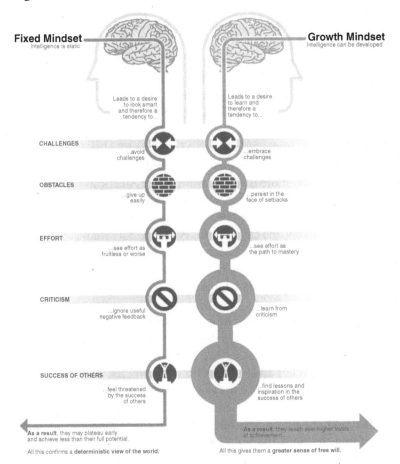

Note. Figure 6.1 contrasts fixed and growth mindsets. The growth mindset is more conducive to academic success. Adapted from *Mindset: The New Psychology of Success*, by C. Dweck, 2006, p. 245. Copyright 2006 by Carol S. Dweck. Graphic by Nigel Holmes. Reproduced with permission.

Letting Go of Stereotypes About Mathematical Ability

David H. Uttal (1997) asked Japanese, Taiwanese, and American mothers—using many different questions—to assess the importance of four aspects of a school child's performance: "effort, natural ability, the difficulty of the schoolwork, and luck or chance" (p. 168). American mothers rated effort as significantly less important than mothers in Asia did, and they also rated innate ability as significantly more important than mothers in Asia did.

Uttal argues persuasively that these differences go a long way toward explaining the differences between American and Asian students' performance on international math assessments. He relates the American mothers' emphasis on innate ability—fixed mindset—to a belief that a child's future can be accurately predicted based on early success or failure. When he asked American and Chinese mothers to say at what point it becomes possible to predict a child's high school math performance, more than one-third of the American mothers but only one-tenth of the Chinese mothers chose the end of elementary school rather than a later time in a child's intellectual development.

Not incidentally, the children surveyed in Uttal's study held beliefs that matched their parents'. Compared to children in Asia, American children are more likely to hold a fixed mindset about mathematics achievement and believe that innate ability determines their performance.

Uttal also proposes that American parents' fixed mindsets may explain two of his other findings. First, he found American parents are satisfied with their children's mediocre performance, whereas parents in Asia express much less satisfaction with their children's higher achievement. Second, American parents and children believe that children in Asia are more talented in mathematics than American children.

Two additional findings complete the picture. American mothers are ambivalent about the value of homework, whereas Japanese and Taiwanese mothers are convinced that homework is important. Consistent with those findings, American fifth graders spent about 4 hours per week doing homework, whereas Japanese and Taiwanese fifth graders spent 6 to 11 hours.

Finally, Uttal cites Stevenson and Stigler's (1992) finding that mindset determines attitudes about errors. People with a fixed mindset tend to view errors as failures, whereas people with a growth mindset view errors as necessary steps in the learning process because they reveal what needs further attention. Stevenson and Stigler found that

American children felt embarrassed when they made errors, whereas Japanese and Chinese children remained largely untroubled by their mistakes.

Uttal sums up his findings, saying, "Perhaps more than any other school subject, mathematics requires effort, diligence, and persistence even in the face of temporary setbacks. A focus on innate ability may discourage children from doing precisely what they must do to succeed in mathematics" (1997, p. 170). I argue that this statement applies to all disciplines, not just mathematics.

I present a brief summary of Uttal's paper in my workshops because the stereotype of the talented Asian mathematician, computer engineer, or other technology professional is so widespread in American culture. Nearly everyone has absorbed this belief to some extent, so it is an effective demonstration of the power of mindset. Mindset determines how much effort we expend and the expectations we have for ourselves, so it logically follows that it is a major factor affecting our performance.

You're Criticizing My Work Because You Think I Can Do Better, Not Because I'm a Lost Cause?

How students respond to criticism gives us further insight into the impact of mindset. When students become aware that their instructors have provided criticism in order to help them improve rather than as a judgment of their ostensibly fixed abilities, they are likelier to use that criticism constructively. Aguilar and colleagues (2014) cite a study by Yeager and colleagues (2013) wherein teachers provided feedback on student essays along with a note that read, "I have high standards but I believe you have the potential to meet them, so I am providing this critical feedback to help you meet those standards." Eighty percent of the students who received the note chose to revise their essays, whereas just 39% chose to do revisions when only criticism was provided. It must be said here that whether or not you have a supportive instructor, criticism can always be used to improve, and you should always submit revisions when given the chance.

IDK

I met a master's degree candidate in LSU's College of Human Sciences and Education, Lorena, who taught math to "gifted" middle school students. She expressed great frustration that her students were performing far, far below their potential. She had written her master's thesis on metacognitive control but was frustrated that she could not persuade her students to think productively about problems that they had not already been taught how to solve. Whenever she gave them challenging problems, they simply wrote "IDK."

Unfamiliar with this shorthand, she asked one student, "What is IDK?"

"I don't know."

She asked another student, who gave her the same response.

"Well if you don't know what it means, why are all of you writing it on your papers?!"

After a few more seconds of confusion, one of the students finally explained to her that "IDK" is an acronym for "I don't know." With unfamiliar problems, the students just refused to try.

Sometimes when students are labeled as gifted, they take on a fixed mindset and may be afraid to try anything that might contradict the idea that they are smart. So instead of facing head-on the confusion that inevitably accompanies meaningful problem-solving, they may instead throw up their hands and say, "IDK." Given this tendency, I want to stress to you how important it is that you tackle challenging tasks that feel threatening. Life is about repeatedly going beyond our perceived limitations. If you never allow yourself to feel the fear and self-doubt that everyone experiences whenever our limits are tested, you will never know what you are capable of achieving.

The Origins and Costs of a Fixed Mindset

The next sections of this chapter explore why many students and instructors hold fixed mindsets, examine some evidence both groups may use to support their fixed mindsets, and discuss the costs of holding on to a fixed mindset.

Why Do Many Students Have a Fixed Mindset?

When you were in elementary school, you and your classmates may have been grouped according to "ability." Everyone knew who the "smart kids" and the "slow kids" were. And I bet when you got to high school the kids in the honors classes were the "smart kids" from elementary school, right? Categorizing students this way almost ensures a fixed mindset. For example, you may have been subtly programmed to think things like "I was just never very good at math," or, "I was always in the slow reading group." Figure 6.1 should make it clear that a fixed mindset can spell disaster, whether a student is judged as "gifted" or "slow." If you have doubts about your intellectual ability in any area, don't let yourself fall into the mindset trap of settling for average grades instead of using metacognition to figure out what you need to do to excel. Conversely, if you consider yourself to have particular strengths in an academic subject, don't fall into the mindset trap of giving less than your best. You should always adopt a growth mindset and know that you can be successful at any task you spend time and effort on, as long as you do it in a metacognitively aware way.

Okay, but, Come On, Aren't Some Students Smarter Than Others?

As I have already mentioned several times, I used to believe wholeheartedly that there are smart students and slow students. Teaching students metacognitive strategies and seeing their astonishing results have completely changed my mind: I now know that there are students who have an arsenal of strategies at their disposal and there are students who don't. It just appears that students using strategies are smart and that students without them are slow.

Now hear this: All students are capable of excelling. You can be certain that very successful students are using effective learning strategies. Some of them absorbed these strategies when they were two or three years old. Some students came by their strategies intuitively and instinctively; these students may not even be able to articulate them as explicit strategies. But, however it happened, these successful students arrived at school, even preschool, with strategies, or at least acquired knowledge, that the other students did not have. So it does appear that there are "smart" students and "slow" students. But in reality, there are only students who have learned strategies or been given prior knowledge and students who haven't. When "slow" students are taught learning strategies, they can do as well as students in the gifted programs.

But Really—What About Mozart? Or Einstein?

Yes, prodigies exist. I would never say that there is no such thing as a prodigy. But no student needs to be anywhere near a prodigy in order to earn As in the vast majority of middle and high school, college, university, or graduate and professional school courses. All students can succeed and make top grades as long as they are consistently using effective strategies. Consider Adam's story.

Mindset Makes Miracles: Adam's Story

Adam enrolled in my colleague Isiah Warner's analytical chemistry course at LSU in the fall of 2005. An engineering major, Adam was due to graduate at the end of that semester, but he needed to pass Professor Warner's class with a grade of C or higher. Unfortunately, he had scored 65, 61, and 61 on the three hourly exams given in the course. Warner told him to contact me. Adam called me on Friday with his final exam looming, scheduled for the following Wednesday. If he did not pass the course, he would not graduate.

We met Monday morning, and I introduced him to several metacognitive strategies including concept mapping, working problems without consulting an example, and pretending to teach the concepts. Then Adam began asking me specific questions about the topics that the test would cover. I explained to him that I had no idea and that he should go speak to his teaching assistant. So Adam went straight from my office to the teaching assistant's office.

Wednesday after the exam, I got a voice mail from Adam. "Dr. McGuire! Those strategies you gave me were sooooo useful! I think the minimum I made on that test was 100!" I thought, "100?! Oh, this poor guy. If he is that deluded about his test performance, he might have scored in the 30s or 40s." So I called Warner. I said to him, "I need to know what Adam made on his final exam because he thinks he did pretty well." I didn't have the nerve to tell Isiah that he thought he made at least 100! Isiah told me, "Hmmm, I don't know what he made. I'll call the grader and find out."

Later that day, Isiah called me back and said, "Saundra, the grader said he made 107, but she *knows* he cheated. She knows he cheated because he came to her office two days before the test and he didn't know anything." I quickly responded, "Well, I'm the one who sent him to her office because he had specific questions about test coverage that I couldn't answer. And it's not really true that he didn't know *anything*. Yes, it's true that he couldn't answer any questions. But he had memorized a lot of information. He just couldn't put it together to answer any questions."

Then I called Adam to find out exactly how he had pulled the rabbit out of the hat. "Adam, I need you to tell me exactly what you did to prepare for this test because they think you cheated." Adam replied, "Ah . . . they think I cheated? I'm so flattered they think I cheated!" Then he explained, "I changed the way I studied. I used to study for his tests the way I studied for my calculus tests. For my calculus tests, I would memorize the solutions to homework problems, and then when I saw a problem on the test, I would identify its type and carry out the steps I had memorized." But my colleague's tests couldn't be hacked that way. His tests featured only applications questions like, "You go into ACME labs and they give you a green solution and they tell you it's killing the men and not the women. What will you do to help?" Because those kinds of questions involve application of concepts, the strategies I had introduced to Adam completely transformed his performance. But if he had had a fixed mindset, rather than a growth mindset, or believed that his Ds indicated inferior ability, Adam never would have been able to turn his performance around.

Once you understand that changing your behavior changes your results, you can switch from a fixed mindset to a growth mindset. Adam's case, along with the other less dramatic cases I have presented, argue strongly that everyone should have a growth mindset.

Four Strategies for Changing Student Mindset

Here I offer four strategies that you can use to help change your mindset:

1. Keep the faith. Recall all of the stories from this book, and see Appendix D for even more examples of students who turned their performance around. Know that if they can do it, you can too.
2. Stand in your power. Make a list of challenges you have already overcome. If you did it then, you can do it now.
3. Learn the neurobiological basis of the growth mindset—namely, brain plasticity.
4. Start easy, end strong. Try to achieve gradual, persistent growth. Wherever possible, never start out with the most difficult problems. Start easy, proceed to intermediate, and save the hardest for last, when you have the skills and the confidence to triumph.

Strategy #1: Keep the Faith

Over the past four chapters, I've told the stories of Dana, Travis, Joshua, and Adam. I've also worked with scores more students with results just as rapid and dramatic. You might also be encouraged by friends who are using learning strategies to transform their grades. Finally, know that I believe in you. There is no reason you can't implement the strategies and have miraculous stories of your own to tell.

Strategy #2: Stand in Your Power

Athletes and performers are particularly quick to understand the power of the strategies because they immediately see that just as they have achieved mastery in athletics or performance through effort they can do the same with intellectual pursuits.

You can take a page from their book and consciously, explicitly recall previous challenges that you have overcome. Go ahead right now and list three of the hardest things you've ever done in your life. Choose at least one example where you saw improvement in 24 hours or less. Choose at least one example that required 3 to 12 months to see real change.

1.

2.

3.

Your 24-hours-or-less example relates to the fast-acting nature of metacognitive strategies, and your 3- to 12-months example relates to the benefits of long-term implementation of the study cycle over multiple semesters.

Let me tell you about my adventures in bowling. I used to be a terrible bowler. Seriously. Have you ever heard of anyone who has ever bowled a score of 0? Well, now you have. I had no idea what to do to get better. I recognized that the paths of my balls were curved, that I was a natural "hook bowler." But I considered myself in good company because I knew that most professionals were hook bowlers. After all, a good hook is more likely to result in a strike! But my ball would curve into one gutter and then into the other gutter when I overcompensated. Suffice it to say, hook bowling was not working for me. When my brother Bobby, a fantastic bowler who has rolled a perfect 300, came to town, he offered to help me with my game. We went to the lanes and got to work. After watching me bowl a few frames Bobby asked me if I used "the arrows." The arrows are marks on the lane that competent bowlers use to aim the ball; good bowlers aim the ball toward the arrows, not the pins. But I replied, "What arrows? What are you talking about? Do you mean the lane decorations?" Bobby put his head in his hands and said, "Oh, no, no, no . . ." Sure enough, once I began aiming my balls toward the arrows, my average jumped to 130. Over time, I even bowled scores of 170 and 180.

Strategy #3: Learn the Neurobiological Basis of the Growth Mindset

We know that the brain is changing all the time. These changes occur in a variety of ways (Kandel, Schwartz, Jessell, Siegelbaum, & Hudspeth, 2013). You may have learned that a synapse is the space between two neurons, or brain cells, across which communication between those two cells occurs. The brain can change via synaptic plasticity, whereby connections between particular synapses are strengthened or weakened through a number of processes. Changes also occur via synaptogenesis (creation of synapses), synaptic pruning (destruction of synapses), and neurogenesis (creation of new neurons). The brain also has the ability to functionally reorganize itself, depending on the stimuli available and the task required. For example, in the brains of deaf people, regions that usually process auditory stimuli have been shown to process visual stimuli instead (Karns, Dow, & Neville, 2012).

The bottom line here is that because your brain is built for change, you are the master of your academic fate.

Strategy #4: Start Easy, End Strong

Consider a study inspired by Seligman and Maier's (1967) groundbreaking study of learned helplessness. Charisse L. Nixon (2007) divided her class into two groups and gave each group three anagrams to solve. (Anagrams are words made up of the same letters but in a different order, like the words *cares* and *races*.) The first group received an easy anagram (bat; the solution is tab), a medium-difficulty anagram (lemon; the solution is melon), and a tough anagram (cinerama; the solution is american), in that order. The second group received two anagrams that were impossible to solve (whirl, slapstick; both have no solution) and a solvable tough anagram (cinerama), in that order. So the two groups received the same third anagram to solve.[1] Most students in the first group solved the third anagram, but very few students in the second group solved it (Nixon, 2007). Nixon inferred that the second group suffered from learned helplessness. Even though the third anagram was solvable, the first two were impossible, leading most of the students in the second group to assume they could not solve it. On the other hand, the students in the first group, who had slowly been gaining confidence in their ability to solve anagrams, performed the task successfully.

This experiment demonstrates why a "sink-or-swim" approach can be so devastating. Even the students who are capable of succeeding become convinced that failure is inevitable.

Take-Home Message: Focus on Effort, Not Ability

Many students come to school with a fixed mindset. Most believe they are smart because they have always been told they are smart and have always made good grades. So if they begin to make lackluster grades on tests, they think they're not smart anymore. In fact, I've heard more than one student say, "Well, maybe I was high school smart, but I'm not college smart." But now you know that's nonsense. Your grades do not reflect how smart you are. They reflect your behavior and the actions you take. Period.

Joshua's Mindset Changed

Remember Joshua, the chemistry student who made 68, 50, and 50 on the first three tests but who scored 97 on his final exam? We've already seen an excerpt of an e-mail he wrote after he triumphed, but let's take a look at part of the first e-mail he sent, reaching out for help:

> Personally, I am not so good at chemistry and unfortunately at this point my grade for that class is reflecting exactly that. (Personal communication, April 6, 2011)

Do you see it? "I am not so good at chemistry" reflects a fixed mindset. But after the course, Joshua wrote,

> I think what I did different was make sidenotes in each chapter, and as I progressed into the next chapter I was able to refer to these notes. I would say that in chemistry, everything builds from the previous topic. (Personal communication, May 13, 2011)

Here, Joshua's language reflects a growth mindset. He attributes his improved performance to his behavior and the specific actions he took.

Next Up

In the next chapter we'll keep exploring the connection between learning and psychological factors, namely motivation and emotion.

Questions to Ask Yourself

1. Before you began reading this chapter, would you say you had a fixed mindset or a growth mindset?
2. Do you think your closest friends and family have mostly fixed mindsets or growth mindsets?
3. List a few ways you can maintain a growth mindset in a fixed-mindset atmosphere.
4. Do you believe your current ability or your future behavior will determine your grades in the future?
5. Do you believe you will be smarter in five years than you are right now? In one year? In a month? Explain.

Note

1. Nixon indicated in personal communication (August 30, 2014) that she did not invent this task but discovered it in a social psychology resource.

7

HOW YOUR EMOTIONS
AFFECT YOUR MOTIVATION
AND LEARNING

"I'm so scared because I don't want to go home and I feel like this test just dropped my average in his class to a C. I really think I have test anxiety. It must be because I know that if I don't get a 4.0 this semester, I'll be going home."

—Marsha C., first-year graduate student on probation,
now Dr. Marsha C., personal communication, May 5, 2008

We have just seen how psychological factors can influence learning and performance. In the next two chapters, we explore these factors further. In this chapter, I lay out some basic information about motivation and emotions, and in chapter 8, I suggest steps that you can take to maximize your own motivation and learning.

What Is Motivation?

Ambrose, Bridges, DiPietro, Lovett, and Norman (2010) define *motivation* as "the personal investment an individual has in reaching a desired state or outcome" (p. 68). As such, "[s]tudents' motivation

Figure 7.1. Motivation Cycle

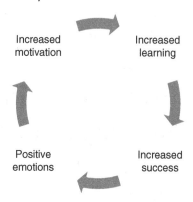

Increased motivation

Increased learning

Positive emotions

Increased success

determines, directs, and sustains what they do to learn" (Ambrose et al., 2010, p. 5). Linda Nilson (2004) writes, "In the academy, the term 'motivating' means stimulating interest in a subject and, therefore, the desire to learn it" (p. 57). Figure 7.1 shows how motivation, success, and positive emotion contribute to a positive feedback loop that drives long-term achievement and goal fulfillment.

What Influences Your Motivation?

Ambrose and colleagues (2010) define three important levers (Figure 7.2) that influence student motivation. The first lever is *value*: What value do you see in the goal? How important is it to you to meet the goal? The second lever is the *nature of the environment*: How helpful is the learning environment? The third lever, one that greatly influences motivation, is *belief in the ability to succeed*: Do you believe you are capable of executing a task? If an individual is unsure whether performing a task will lead to a positive outcome, that person tends to be unmotivated.

Many students do not appear to be motivated, but those students are indeed motivated to engage in many activities. They are motivated to level up in video games, text friends, tweet about the latest viral

Figure 7.2. Three Levers Influencing Student Motivation

1. **Value.** *How important do I find this goal?*

2. **Nature of the environment.** *Do I feel supported or unsupported?*

3. **Belief in the ability to succeed.** *Do I believe I can design and follow a course of action to meet this goal?*

Note. Figure 7.2 lists Ambrose and colleagues' (2010) three important levers affecting student motivation. In order to feel motivated, students must find value in a goal, be in a supportive environment, and/or believe they can reach the goal.

news, go to sports games, and pursue any number of socially relevant or recreational goals. Why are they motivated to do those things? They see value in those goals, feel very supported by their peers to pursue them, and have confidence, borne of past experience, that they will be successful (Figure 7.2).

Why Is It So Hard to Stay Motivated?

Optimal learning requires a partnership between teachers and learners; similarly, behavior that increases or decreases student motivation can come from instructors or students. In the following section, I lay out the obstacles to student success from each side of the partnership (Figures 7.3 and 7.4).

Student-Related Obstacles to Motivation

These days, myriad demands compete for students' time and energy (Figure 7.3). Many students tend to work long hours and do not get enough rest or exercise, let alone proper nutrition. A great deal of students also lack time management and learning strategies, and an increasing proportion come to campus with diagnoses of attention deficit hyperactivity disorder (ADHD) or one or more learning disabilities. As a result, students often feel that they are working as hard as they can and so deserve good grades. Furthermore, many students pursue higher education primarily for credentials in order to secure better-paying,

Figure 7.3. Student-Related Obstacles to Motivation

- Students may work long hours.

- Students may have ADHD or related diagnoses.

- Students may be interested primarily in credentials.

- Students may feel As and Bs are their just rewards for consistent attendance.

- Students may not know how to manage their time.

- Students may have few learning strategies.

Note. Figure 7.3 lists reasons that today's students may be more difficult to motivate than students in the past.

more professionally rewarding jobs. They do not yet believe that the value of earning a degree lies in fully absorbing the information presented in courses required by the degree.

If you fall into one of these categories, I hope this book will convince you that you can overcome these obstacles to deep, lasting learning.

Faculty-Related Obstacles to Student Motivation

A supportive learning environment is the second of Ambrose and colleagues' (2010) three factors that influence student motivation

Figure 7.4. Faculty-Related Obstacles to Student Motivation

- The classroom environment is daunting or unsupportive.

- Faculty expectations are unclear.

- Students are paralyzed by a sink-or-swim course structure.

Note. Figure 7.4 lists reasons for low student motivation that faculty have the power to change.

(Figure 7.2). Figure 7.4 asserts that an unsupportive environment is the number one obstacle to student motivation.

When instructors' expectations of students are unclear, student motivation suffers because without clear learning goals, students cannot effectively plan a course of action to meet those goals. In my experience, instructors can be all over the map in terms of their expectations for students. Some ask students to demonstrate very precise and accurate memorization of detailed facts, others look primarily for high-level mastery and creative application of concepts, and most fall somewhere in between those extremes. If you are unclear about expectations in a particular class, do your best to gather that information from as many sources as you can. Scrutinize the syllabus, interview past students, and show up to the instructor's office hours as often as you can with clear, relevant questions. It's important to come prepared to meetings with your instructors because you do not want to be perceived as an annoyance by someone who is assigning your grades.

Eric Hobson (2001) studied sources of positive and negative motivation among a population of students at a college of pharmacy. He found that if faculty held the attitude that everybody in the course could learn and excel, then students were highly motivated. But if the students heard the equivalent of, "Look to your left, look to your right. Two of you are not going to be here in three weeks," then students became discouraged. The instructor's attitude, among six other factors, accounted for a full 27% of students' positive motivation and a whopping 32% of students' negative motivation (Hobson, 2001).

I once knew of a professor who would tell his students on the first day of class, "I hope you've signed up for enough hours so that when you have to drop this class you won't go under the minimum number of hours required to be a full-time student and lose your financial aid." This professor did not create a supportive learning environment or motivate most of his students to pursue success in his course. In fact, after hearing this statement on the first day of class, many students went straight to their adviser to drop the course. If you find yourself in a similar situation, know that with enough tenacity and commitment to using the strategies in this book, you can also be successful in a sink-or-swim academic environment.

The Course Syllabus:
A Road Map to Instructor Expectations

In the previous section, I encouraged you to use the syllabus to deduce your instructor's expectations. Now I will explain exactly how to do that. The course syllabus is the document that provides information about course expectations, homework assignments, required readings, test dates, and term projects. There is also valuable information about the instructor's office hours and how to contact the instructor. All instructors expect that you will be thoroughly familiar with the syllabus and will not ask them questions that you could have answered yourself if only you had read it carefully (Gardner, Jewler, & Barefoot, 2009).

Here's an activity that will help you to become more familiar with the syllabus for each of your courses. Do this whether or not your instructor has spent time in class reviewing the syllabus.

1. Write out all of the questions you have about the course. These might include: How many tests will there be, and what dates will they be on? Will I have an opportunity for extra credit? What is the grading scale for the course? Is the final examination cumulative (covering the whole course) or will it be just on the material covered since the last class exam? When and where are my instructor's office hours? Write down every question you think you might have, leaving space to write the answers.

2. Go through the syllabus looking for answers to each of your questions, and write the answers in the space you provided for yourself. For all unanswered questions, visit your instructor's office hours within the first week of class to get those answers. Begin the meeting by telling your instructor that you have thoroughly studied the syllabus but you still have a few questions. Emphasize that you are determined to do everything you can to learn the course material and meet all of the course requirements at the highest level. If you do this, you will be in a great position to do very well in the course *and* your instructor will know that you are a serious student who will put time

and effort into excelling. Making a positive impression on the instructor can reap great rewards as the course proceeds.

Instructors Are Human Beings With Emotions Too

Instructors have families, hobbies, and interests, just like you do. As long as you maintain appropriate professional distance, there is nothing wrong with making small talk with an instructor about an interest of yours like a sport, a particular author or composer, a film genre, or a region of the world. Who knows? The instructor may share your interest. Use your judgment to determine which instructors are more open to building rapport this way and which ones might prefer to keep it strictly business. Things may be different depending on the day and the demands on the instructor's time. Do your best not to take anything personally. But above all, do not be intimidated by instructors. Their lives are filled with joys, sorrows, stresses, successes, and failures, just like anybody else's. Don't put them on a pedestal, but do treat them with consideration and respect, the way you would want to be treated if you were in their position. Although unsympathetic instructors do exist, please know that the vast majority of them want to get to know you and are very interested in doing what they can to ensure your success.

Go to Office Hours Regularly Throughout the Semester

You shouldn't stop at seeing your instructor to discuss the course syllabus. Go to office hours regularly throughout the semester. Your instructor *wants* to see you there. Let's say you are taking four or five courses during a particular semester. If you go see each instructor every two weeks, that's approximately two appointments per week. Now, if you are pressed for time and are doing extremely well in a class, don't just go to office hours for the sake of checking a box. But if you could be doing better in a class, and if you have the time and can show up prepared, then you should attend office hours like clockwork. No question. In doing so, you will build valuable relationships with potential mentors or recommendation letter writers. Aim to make your instructors part of your future professional network. Having professors in your corner feels great, and it boosts both motivation and learning.

Sydnie's Story: The Power of Encouragement

I met Sydnie on September 23, 2013, the morning that I gave a presentation about metacognitive learning strategies to an honors-level general chemistry class at LSU. I arrived about an hour early, as I usually do, and there was Sydnie, alone in the classroom, sitting in the front row. She spotted me and brightly asked, "Are you going to teach us today?"

"Yes!" I replied.

"What are you going to talk about?" she asked.

"I'm going to talk about learning strategies. How are you doing in this class?" I inquired.

Sydnie proudly reported, "Oh, I'm doing great! I did really well on the first exam. I made a 97.5, but I didn't think I had done that well." My attention sharpened. I knew that the test had 150 available points, so in a carefully positive tone, I said, "Oh! Well, the test had a total of 150 points, so do you know if you made 97.5 out of 150, or 97.5%?" After a sharp intake of breath, Sydnie said in a panicked tone, "I don't know. Let me check." In a flash, her laptop was open and her fingers began flying. I heard the clickety-clack of the keys as she checked the course website. All of a sudden I saw big tears begin to flow down Sydnie's cheeks. Immediately I reassured her, "No, no, don't get discouraged yet! We're going to talk about some things that will turn your chemistry grade around." Dejected, she said, "No, you don't understand. I made a D on my first calculus test too." I could see that she was beyond demoralized, so I said, "Don't worry about that either. We're going to talk about some ideas today that will help you make As on the next tests in both of those courses." Because I could see she was so distressed that she needed additional encouragement, I asked her to visit my office after class. During our meeting I didn't give her any additional learning strategies, but I did tell her that because I could see how motivated she was to use the strategies, I had complete confidence that she would ace her next tests. I let her know that I would be available if she needed any help at all. In that short meeting, I increased Sydnie's belief in herself by emphasizing that I had faith in her ability to excel, and I created a supportive learning environment. By the time she left my office she had acquired effective learning strategies as well as the motivation to use them!

Sydnie finished the semester with a 4.0 GPA (see Figure 7.5) and attributed her success to previewing, reviewing, and treating her homework assignments as assessment opportunities. She also earned a 4.0 GPA in her next semester and finished her first year in college with a perfect GPA despite having started with Ds on her first two undergraduate exams. Sydnie's grades attest to the power of encouragement, motivation, and metacognitive learning strategies to fuel the cycle depicted in Figure 7.1. Sydnie graduated from LSU in spring 2017 with a 3.5 cumulative GPA and is a very competitive candidate for medical school.

Figure 7.5 Sydnie's First-Semester Exam Scores

General chemistry: 65, **95, 90, 70, 96 (final)**

Calculus: 64, **100, 97, 96, 90, 93 (final)**

Note. Sydnie's dramatic turnaround at the beginning of her first semester demonstrates the power of encouragement, motivation, and learning strategies. Bold-faced numbers represent grades Sydnie earned after being exposed to metacognitive strategies.

What You Can Do to Boost Your Motivation, Stay Positive, and Increase Your Learning

The next chapter presents strategies you can use to stay motivated and pumped up about learning.

An Activity for You

1. If you lack motivation to spend time on academic pursuits, take five minutes to freewrite about why.

8

WHAT YOU CAN DO TO BOOST YOUR MOTIVATION, POSITIVE EMOTIONS, AND LEARNING

"This was such an amazing way to keep me motivated. After experimenting with these strategies, I would definitely advise a new student at [the University of Rhode Island] next year to not slack off. It may seem pointless to do a few problems every night. It may seem silly to talk out loud as if you are the one teaching the material. It may seem like a lot of work to read over your notes and the textbook a little at a time. Those are all things I used to believe but, in the long run it is much more beneficial and will relieve a lot more stress if you do these things."

—Anonymous feedback from University of Rhode Island
undergraduates after a presentation on metacognition, May 5, 2017

This chapter lists five strategies that you can use to boost your motivation and learning. All of the strategies are listed in Figure 8.1. After laying out the strategies, we will talk about what to do if you feel that the strategies just aren't working for you or you aren't getting the results you want.

Strategy #1: Use the Learning Strategies!

The bulk of your efforts should go toward implementing the learning strategies presented in chapter 5. Recall the cycle depicted in Figure 7.1. Increased success leads to positive emotions, which, in turn, lead to increased motivation. In other words, academic success, brought about by implementing the learning strategies, is primary. This chapter describes how you can create a mental and emotional environment that will optimally support your learning efforts.

Strategies #2, 3, and 4: Adopt a Growth Mindset, Monitor Self-Talk, and Attribute Results to Actions

Appendix B lists recommended books and websites for students, and Carol Dweck's (2006) book *Mindset* is near the top of the list. What if you don't have any extra time to read the book? You can visit Dweck's website (www.mindsetonline.com) to discover more and take an online assessment. However it happens, you must be convinced that the most powerful influence on your grades is your behavior, not your innate intelligence or talent. When you believe success is possible, motivation increases.

Monitoring and adjusting self-talk is another great way to increase motivation. Self-talk comprises all of someone's thoughts directed toward himself or herself. For example, perhaps Bob is trying to give his car a tune-up and forgets to replace the oil cap before starting the engine. As a result, Bob makes a big mess. The thought that flies across Bob's mind might be, "Ugh! How could you have done something so colossally stupid?!" Or it might be, "Wow. I must be really tired. I remember when this happened to my good buddy Janet. We'll have a laugh about it later."

Self-talk constantly occupies our minds. If the majority of those thoughts are negative and self-destructive, they can negatively impact our learning efforts (Hirsch, 2001). Conversely, if our self-talk is compassionate and encouraging, it can make learning easier.

Suppose Suzanne studied very hard for the second exam in her Twentieth-Century Continental Philosophy course, but when the exam is returned to her, it is covered in red with "D" at the top. Suzanne might think, "No matter how hard I study, I'll never be good at this stuff. I must be so stupid." This response is extremely common. But a healthier, more robust response to failure is possible. Suzanne could say to herself, "Wow! Well, I guess the methods and strategies I used for that test didn't work. My next assignment will be a great opportunity to try some new things that might work better." Cultivating a growth mindset and developing healthy self-talk go hand in hand.

Pay attention to your self-talk, perhaps for a 24-hour period. During this observation period, don't try to change anything; rather, you should just pay attention and maintain awareness. Then, once you've taken your self-talk temperature, you can begin to challenge one unhelpful thought out of 10. On hearing self-talk like, "I'll never get this stuff," you might respond, "Never say never. I have new things I can try." Or you might respond, "That guy David failed his first two tests and made an A on the third. Why not me?" Another response might be, "Yes, I will get this stuff if I pay attention now and keep using the strategies and putting in the time." Effective responses to negative self-talk usually embody a spirit of curiosity or gentle determination. Anything violent or punitive is probably coming from the place that produced the negative self-talk to begin with. Making self-talk more positive should not be an onerous, endless chore for you. It should happen gently and gradually so that you can maintain your new behavior.

In addition to your mindset and self-talk, you should examine how you explain your successes and failures. If you attribute your successes to plain dumb luck or Kelly's last-minute help and you attribute your failures to your "inexorable stupidity," you will not be a confident, empowered learner. However, if you attribute both your successes and failures to your behavior, which you can control, then you will know what to do to maintain or increase your success and reverse your failures. Ask yourself why you did not do as well on an exam, a paper, or a project as you wanted to or thought you would. Encourage yourself to locate the answers in your own behavior and attitudes, rather than external circumstances. Consider the possibility that you hold the power to change your results by changing your behavior.

Strategy #5: Rest, Nutrition, and Exercise: Good for the Body, Good for the Brain

More and more, with each passing year, students are expected to push themselves past their limits. Consequently, you might be tempted to save time by eating mostly fast foods, skimping on sleep, and diminishing extracurricular activities like exercise and hobbies. But the brain is part of the body. You should try to exercise regularly and maintain at least the minimum level of physical fitness you need to support your learning efforts (Medina, 2008).

All-nighters may be necessary evils a couple of times per semester, but persistent sleep deprivation is one of the fastest ways to undermine your health and GPA. Some students might need only four hours a night, but some students need nine. You should figure out the minimum amount of sleep you need and make sure to consistently get it. When you cannot get enough sleep or are feeling stressed out, simple techniques like deep breathing or guided relaxation have proven very effective in helping to decrease unhealthy levels of anxiety (see Appendix B). Professionals at the campus mental health center can also teach you these techniques.

Nutrition is as important to the brain as oxygen and rest are. Doing an Internet search for "recipes for busy college students" will yield a plethora of quick and simple recipes that will keep you alert and fueled for success.

Figure 8.1. Five Strategies Students Can Use to Increase Motivation

1. Use the learning strategies.

2. Cultivate a mindset that your intelligence can grow.

3. Engage in positive, healthy self-talk.

4. Attribute positive and negative results to your behavior, not external circumstances.

5. Get adequate rest, nutrition, and exercise.

Figure 8.1 summarizes the five strategies presented in this chapter for staying motivated, healthy, and joyful during your academic journey.

What to Do When All Else Fails

In my work with students over the years, I have found that a small percentage find it difficult to implement the strategies and find success. If, after trying the strategies for a few weeks, you feel like you fall into this category, this section is for you.

Have You Owned Your Part?

Pay close attention to your thoughts. With whom do you find fault when things do not go as you would like? If, most of the time, you find yourself blaming others or external circumstances, it may be time to reevaluate your perspective. Everything that goes wrong in a person's life, no matter who that person is, can be explained by referring to external circumstances. For example, if I get drenched walking to my car after office hours because I forgot my umbrella, I could say that a student's unexpected visit made me forget it. But instead of placing the responsibility for my wet socks on the student's shoulders, I might find it more empowering to locate the responsibility in my own behavior, so that I can change it in the future. *I* got distracted; *I* forgot my umbrella; next time, as soon as I notice it's raining, *I* can hang it on the hook right next to my office door as a reminder to myself. Even if it's *really* tempting to blame outside circumstances— perhaps a fire alarm or some other hugely startling event distracted me—it is still true that *I* forgot my umbrella. I shouldn't beat myself up for forgetting because it's understandable why it happened. But I must still take *responsibility*. That way, I have maximum power over what happens to me. There is limit to that power—I cannot control the weather—but I can still do my best to watch the forecasts and prepare myself for every foreseeable circumstance. In other words, no one is completely in control of his or her fate, but taking responsibility is one way each person can maximize his or her contribution to his or her own happiness.

Please note that I am in no way suggesting that victims of abuse, assault, harassment, or neglect are in any way responsible for the crimes committed against them. Nor am I suggesting that students who live through a traumatic event, including the death of a loved one or a debilitating illness, have a responsibility to soldier on no matter what. In cases like these, one's responsibility is to take care of one's self, reach out for support to the best of one's ability, and prioritize recovery and healing, even if it means taking some time off from school. I have shared many stories of resilient students overcoming daunting circumstances in order to inspire you, not to shame you into thinking that if you require more time or support to regain your footing after similar events you are somehow inadequate. Victim blaming is never acceptable. Sometimes the answer to the question, "Have you owned your part?" is "Yes, and then some."

Work, Work, Work, Work, Work

Another reason that some students may have trouble successfully implementing learning strategies is an overloaded work schedule. There are students who are employed for so many hours, are taking so many credits, and have so many other responsibilities that they do not actually have time to use any of the strategies. For example, a student with 3 children who is working 40 hours a week and taking 21 credit hours has set himself up for failure. If you are such a student, you should take fewer hours or cut back on your work hours if you can. If you don't think that you can make it work financially, think again. It will be *very* expensive for you to fail your courses. Figure out a way to make it work so that you have a shot at the success you deserve.

Slow and Steady Wins the Race

Sometimes there is just too big a gap between the skills required to succeed in a particular course and the skills that you currently have. For example, if you have not mastered fractions, decimals, or percentages, you will find it exceedingly difficult to succeed in general chemistry. You should, without any shame, take a preparatory course and return to the more advanced course later. If you think this is not a viable option because it will delay your graduation, consider that failing courses also delays graduation. Know yourself, and set yourself up for success. Do not, however, go too far in the other direction and think that just because you floundered in second-semester calculus you can't take economics. If you are unsure, talk to supportive academic advisers who can help you decide when it's okay to have a skills gap and when it might be a problem.

The Bottom Line: How You Feel Matters

In the previous three chapters, we have discussed a range of influences that can affect learning much more powerfully than any purely intellectual factors. I hope you will use the suggestions in this chapter and chapter 7 to make school and learning as fun and exciting for yourself as possible.

Questions to Ask Yourself

1. Is my self-talk generally positive or negative?
2. What can I do to make my self-talk more helpful?
3. How much sleep do I need?
4. How many times a week would I like to try to exercise?
5. How much cooking can I realistically do?
6. How will I nourish myself when cooking is not possible?
7. Have I acknowledged the role of feelings in my academic success? Is it important to me that I feel good, or am I convinced that feeling terrible means I am making a sacrifice necessary for academic success?
8. List three people you can talk to when you are feeling blue.

9

TIME MANAGEMENT, TEST TAKING, AND STRESS REDUCTION

"I just want to thank you again for all your help! I came into your office three weeks ago after getting a 46/80 on my first biochemistry exam. I was so discouraged and felt that I was doing all that I could to succeed in the class. You really opened my eyes to new ways of managing my time and helped me find ways to relieve some of the unwanted stress I was carrying around, which was affecting my studying. I just got back my second test grade and I received an 80/80; a perfect score!"

—Nikole V., first-year SUNY Brockport student, personal communication to Dr. Algernon Kelley, October 17, 2014

Time Is Money: Terrific Time Management Tips

Implementing effective learning strategies requires that you invest the necessary time. Because many students (and instructors!) these days spend too much time engaging in social media, gaming, or playing with the latest irresistible app, simple time management strategies will help you use your time optimally. Even if you don't have a Snapchat addiction, perhaps you are used to loading up your schedule with extracurricular activities including sports, student organizations, performing arts projects, and community service because, until now, you have only needed 6 to 10 hours a week of focused study to do well in all of your classes. If so, time management strategies will be extremely useful for you. Courses in higher education are often extremely fast-paced and require a lot of intellectual independence, and that is why it is so common for first-year students (including first-year graduate and professional students) to fall behind and perform poorly on their first tests. Time management strategies can save you from this fate.

Time Management Tip 1:
Keep a Semester Calendar Showing Major Events

Many of you may have heard this illustration before: Imagine you have a big bucket, and your task is to fill it with some water, some smaller rocks, some big rocks, and some sand, not necessarily in that order. In what order would you place the items in the bucket? Many people respond that they would put in the big rocks first, followed by the smaller rocks, the sand, and finally the water. That makes sense, right? The biggest and most unwieldy things go in first, and the most flexible, maneuverable thing goes in last.

So it is with time management. You must make sure your schedule can accommodate major projects and tasks before scheduling lower priority obligations. But how can you know which major events and projects to prioritize? You need an overall big picture. For time management success, you should create a semester calendar that shows all 16 to 20 weeks of the term on one page. Think of it as Semester-at-a-Glance. (Helpful templates for semester-at-a-glance and week-at-a-glance calendars can be found on many websites.) You should then use your course syllabi to enter all major tests, quizzes, papers, projects, and social events on this calendar. Table 9.1 shows one section of an example of such a calendar. You can see that this student has a major physics exam the Monday after a big anniversary celebration for her parents. Moreover, the celebration occurs after a week packed with projects. Accordingly, she will need to start studying for that physics exam two weeks before the exam date. The semester calendar can and should be updated as more information arrives.

Table 9.1. Section of a Semester-at-a-Glance Calendar

Week	MON	TUE	WED	THU	FRI	SAT	SUN
...	...	...	...	...	...	...	...
Week 3		Calculus quiz	Lit. presentation		Figure-drawing project	Parents' 40th anniv!!!	Parents' 40th anniv!!!
Week 4	Physics exam			German exam		Billy's concert	
Week 5	Calculus exam			Lit. quiz			
Week 6		Physics quiz			German quiz	NYC!!	NYC!!
...	...	...	...	...	...	...	...

Note. For effective time management, students should keep one master calendar showing all of the weeks of the semester on one page. This figure displays a section of such a calendar, showing four weeks, early in the semester, in the life of this first-year physics major.

Time Management Tip 2:
Keep a Weekly Calendar With All Scheduled Activities

Once you have a semester calendar showing the big picture, you can use a weekly calendar to get specific and schedule your time on an hourly basis. Include classes, work, extracurricular activities, social time, intense study sessions, grocery shopping, laundry, and sleep time on your weekly schedule. See Table 9.2 for an example of a weekly calendar. This student is carrying 12 credit hours. You can see that he has scheduled sufficient study time for all four of his classes without sacrificing a weekly hangout with his buddies and seven hours of sleep nightly. Of course, this schedule may be a walk in the park compared to the course loads and work schedules that some of you are contending with. No matter how heavy the load, however, organizational tools like these will promote greater success.

Time Management Tip 3:
Learn to Say You Have an Appointment

Once you have filled out your weekly calendars, there may be blocks of free time. You should learn to think of that time as booked too. During those hours, you "have an appointment with yourself."

Consider the following scenario: Angela, a first-semester student in the College of Music, has just filled out her weekly calendar. Max, Angela's dear friend from high school, runs into her and says with a huge grin on his face, "Angela! What are you doing Sunday at 3:00 p.m.?" Angela looks at her schedule; there's nothing there for Sunday at 3:00 p.m., so she says, "Nothing. Why?" Max responds, "Oh, I'm dying to go look at some rare wildlife on the lake across town!" Now, Angela doesn't want to go watch ducks, but she also doesn't want to disappoint her friend, and she's already told him she's free. Unless Angela has strong boundaries, she might end up at the lake instead of studying for an important advanced theory exam or engaging in an activity she truly enjoys. Let's rewind this scenario and see how it might go after Angela learns Tip 3:

"Angela! What are you doing Sunday at 3:00 p.m.?"

"Oh, I have an appointment. Why do you ask?"

"Well, I wanted to go watch wildlife across town with you."

"I'm so sorry, Max. I've got a prior obligation."

Angela has effectively protected her time, and Max is not offended. Win-win. But let's say Max had free tickets to *Hamilton* instead of an offer to ogle mallards. Angela could easily tell him that she'll reschedule her appointment. This approach enables you to protect your time and to use it in the most efficient and enjoyable ways possible. Of course, your ultimate goal might be to firmly and truthfully communicate your choices without feeling guilty or defensive. But until you get there, use Tip 3.

Time Management Tip 4:
Start Homework Assignments as Soon as They Are Given

In high school, most students find that they do not need to think about homework until the due date is approaching. But you should begin homework as soon as it is assigned and do it in increments each day. This way, you have time to apply the homework strategies and engage deeply with the material.

In my individual consultations with students, there comes a time when I ask, "When do you usually begin your homework?" You will not be surprised to hear that they usually say, "I start my homework the day before it's due."

"When you start the day before, what is your main goal?" I ask.

"To get it finished," comes the predictable response.

I call that being in "git-'er-done mode." I explain to students that if they're in git-'er-done mode, they are not going to be able to make themselves approach the homework meaningfully because it does take time to apply the learning strategies. I explain to students that they must begin their homework the day it is assigned and do the problems two or three at a time, completing about a fifth of the problems each day. If you do your homework in this way, you give yourself the time you need to discover and apply the problem-solving strategies that work best for you.

In fact, in my fall 2010 general chemistry class at LSU, I performed a survey after the first exam. When I asked the students who earned As, "What did you do?" many of them reported that they began the homework the day it was assigned and did a few problems at a time. When I asked the students who made Ds and Fs, "What do you wish you had

Table 9.2. Week-at-a-Glance Calendar

Hours	MON	TUE	WED	THU	FRI	SAT	SUN
7–8 a.m.	Breakfast	Gym	Breakfast	Sleep	Gym	Sleep	Sleep
8–9 a.m.	ISS French	Gym	Groceries	Breakfast	Gym	Sleep	Sleep
9–10 a.m.		Breakfast	Stat preview	ISS GM	Breakfast	ISS French	Breakfast
10–11 a.m.	Stat		Stat	ISS French	Statistics		
11 a.m.–12 p.m.	Stat review Econ preview	French preview	Stat review Econ preview	French preview	Stat review	ISS Stat	Stud. Gov't
12–1 p.m.	Lunch	French	Lunch	French	Lunch	ISS Econ	Stud. Gov't
1–2 p.m.	ISS Stat	French	ISS GM	French	ISS Econ	Lunch	Stud. Gov't
2–3 p.m.	ISS Stat	French review, ISS	ISS Econ	French review/ lunch	ISS Econ	Lunch	
3–4 p.m.	Econ	Lunch	Econ	Lunch	Econ	ISS GM	ISS Econ
4–5 p.m.	Econ review	ISS GM	Dinner	ISS GM	Dinner	Relax	ISS Stat

5–6 p.m.	Dinner	Dinner	Dinner	GM	Dinner	Relax	Dinner
6–7 p.m.	Dinner	Dinner	ISS French	Snack	Friends & family	Hang out	Dinner
7–8 p.m.	ISS Econ	Dinner	ISS Stat	Soccer	Friends & family	Hang out	Movie
8–9 p.m.	ISS GM	ISS French	ISS GM	Soccer	ISS French	Hang out	Movie
9–10 p.m.	Friends & family	ISS Stat	Friends & family	Dinner	ISS GM	Hang out	Movie
10–11 p.m.	Laundry	Friends & family	Wind down	Dinner	Wind down	Hang out	Wind down
11 p.m.–12 a.m.	Wind down	Wind down	Wind down	Wind down	Wind down	Hang out	Wind down

ISS = Intense Study Session; Stat = Statistics; Econ = Economics; GM = Global Marketing; Stud. Gov't = Student Government

Note. Table 9.2 displays a weekly calendar for a hypothetical economics major. This student has scheduled time for his classes, extracurricular activities, errands, and friends and family, and he still comfortably has time for 26 hours of intense study sessions per week.

done?" many responded that they had started the homework too late and wished they had begun it sooner.

When I'm working one-on-one or talking to groups of students, I tell them, "If you start the homework too late, you won't be able to absorb the material because your brain is saying, 'We don't have time to figure this stuff out; just use the solutions manual!'" You need to understand that you are preparing for your next exam each and every day, using homework assignments and other self-assigned tasks as tools. The semester calendar and weekly calendar help you appropriately focus your efforts. If you look at your calendar at the beginning of the semester and see that your first big exam is two to three weeks later, you can devise a study schedule for that exam, spend adequate time on homework assignments, and stay on track.

Keep in mind that small chunks of time are just as useful as big chunks where homework is concerned. Consider another lesson that we can learn from the story about filling our time bucket with large rocks, smaller rocks, sand, and water: No matter how many rocks or how much sand we've packed in, there are likely still pockets of air here and there for the water to fill. Five or 10 minutes is enough time to learn the conjugation of an important verb in a difficult tense, for example.

Time Management Tip 5:
Prioritize According to Your Needs and Wants

Once you have your semester and weekly calendars and you have learned to protect your time, the only thing left is to put first things first. Invariably we schedule more than we can actually accomplish, so the time will come when you will have to decide: Do I go grocery shopping or do I do a fourth intense study session? Do I go hang out with my buddies or do I try to go to sleep early? The right answers to these questions are not at all obvious. You must get to know yourself, to understand when it's better to push through and keep working and when you'd be better off blowing off steam or catching a nap. As you figure out your own needs, you will make mistakes and need to forgive yourself. Remember that optimizing time management is a lifelong process for all of us and that every step we take has tangible future benefits.

Time Management Tips Roundup

- Keep a semester calendar (Table 9.1).
- Keep a weekly calendar that includes activities (Table 9.2).
- Commit to at least 20 to 25 hours of study time each week, utilizing intense study sessions (Table 9.2).
- Guard precious free time with your life.
- Start homework as early as possible.
- Prioritize according to your needs and wants.

Super Exam Preparation Tips

Many students think that preparing for a test means memorizing information the night before or rereading the information until their brain convinces them, "I've got it!" when that's just wishful thinking. The idea that test preparation begins from day one of class is foreign to most students. Here are strategies you can use to make sure you are prepared to conquer your exams:

- Create a test-preparation schedule.
- Use effective learning strategies from day one.
- Determine exactly what the test will cover, and practice teaching that information to an audience—either real or imaginary—until you can do it flawlessly.
- Determine what types of questions will be asked. Preparing for a multiple-choice test is different from preparing for an essay test. If you might have to answer an essay question about the precipitating events of World War II, practice writing that essay. If you know you could be asked to solve three different types of Fourier transform problems, spend time mastering each type.
- Organize the information by preparing charts, outlines, or a study guide.
- Make up a practice test from information in your notes and the textbook.

In the Testing Room: What to Do on Test Day

I have seen many examples of students who were well prepared for a test, but who performed poorly because they failed to utilize the following test-taking skills:

- Write down formulas you may need on the exam before you begin.
- Read the directions *very* carefully, listen for additional directions, and ask for clarification.
- Survey the exam and budget your time.
- Begin with the easiest questions and work your way up to the harder ones. This will build confidence and bring more information to your mind.
- Expect memory blocks and recognize that the information will come back to you if you move on to other questions.
- Perform deep-breathing exercises to relax; use positive self-talk.
- Remain confident that if you have prepared well you will do well.

What to Do After the Test Is Returned

Most students don't realize how much valuable information their returned tests contain. When many students get a test back, they typically put it out of sight, especially if the grade is lower than they anticipated. But you should analyze all of your returned tests and quizzes, reflect on what you missed and why, and develop a plan for improvement. One popular technique for analyzing returned exams is called "exam wrappers." Get out a blank sheet of paper and draw two horizontal lines, dividing it into thirds. In the top third, write down exactly how you prepared for the exam. In the middle third, describe the kinds of mistakes you made and why. At the bottom, explain how you will prepare differently for the next exam. Reflecting on what went wrong and implementing strategies to prevent future errors guarantee improvement in any area.

Use Your Campus Learning Center: The Professionals There Would Love to Be of Service

In this chapter, we've taken a look at a few of the strategies that learning specialists routinely teach students who visit their campus learning center. If your campus has a learning center (and most do), the professionals there can serve as transformative partners in the learning process. Their chosen careers reflect a desire to serve students in their quest for deep, lasting, meaningful learning. Find out where they are on your campus and use them as much as you can.

To find your campus learning center, visit your institution's website and search for "tutoring" even if you are not actually looking for tutoring. The search results should include a link to the learning center. You can also ask your academic adviser to point you to the center.

Those of you who are looking for on-campus employment should be aware that campus learning centers are always looking for students with great learning strategies to serve as tutors and mentors for other students. The pay is usually well above minimum wage. You will be not only rewarded financially but also enjoy the satisfaction of knowing you have helped others succeed.

Activities for You

1. Take 10 minutes to work on your Semester-at-a-Glance calendar. After 10 minutes, feel free to continue; if you'd rather not, spend another 10 minutes on it later today or tomorrow.
2. Take 10 minutes to work on your Week-at-a-Glance calendar. After 10 minutes, feel free to continue; if you'd rather not, spend another 10 minutes on it later today or tomorrow.
3. Imagine a friend you find it hard to say no to has asked you to do something you'd rather not do. Practice telling this person you have an appointment. Once you have that mastered, you might practice telling him or her that you would prefer to spend time studying, recharging by yourself, or engaging in some other activity, whatever is truest for you.

10

TRY THE STRATEGIES AND
HAVE FUN!

In the previous chapters, I have presented quite a few strategies, but I hope the underlying principles are clear:

- You must believe you can be successful.
- You must determine exactly what is expected of you.
- You must have an arsenal of effective learning strategies.

Each of the strategies presented in this book fulfills one of those three aims.

In this chapter, we will look at how you can go about discovering which strategies work best for you.

No Right or Wrong Approaches, Just Use the Scientific Method

There is no right or wrong way to become a better learner. The best way to find out what works for you is to dive right in and see which strategies you enjoy the most.

Let's recall the scientific method, which you may have learned in middle or high school: Make observations and pose a question, create a hypothesis based on those observations, experiment to test your hypothesis, draw conclusions based on your results, revise the hypothesis according to your results, design new experiments, and continue the process until you have the answers you're looking for. That's exactly the process I went through to determine which strategies to present in this book.

So why not use the scientific method yourself? Make a prediction about which strategies will work best for you based on how you intuitively responded to reading about them. Experiment by trying those strategies out for three weeks. Look at your academic results and decide whether you need to adjust your approach. If you think you do, choose additional strategies that you believe will effectively supplement your efforts. Try that combination of strategies for a couple of weeks and see how it goes. Refine your arsenal of strategies even further. Keep at it until you are entirely satisfied with your academic performance and, more importantly, the depth of your learning.

Different Strategies for Different Classes

Keep in mind that if a strategy does not work for one class, that doesn't mean it won't work for another. You will learn over time which tools and strategies work best with which types of classes. For example, flashcards may work best in courses that require lots of memorization, whereas mapping may work better in courses that focus on application of concepts (see Appendix F). Certainly, there will be many courses that require two, three, or more strategies and tools. You can experiment and use different approaches for different subjects until you find success in all of them.

Exercise: Commit to Action

In the following space, please write down two to three strategies that you will begin using as soon as possible. The sooner you start, the sooner you will be on the path to independent, self-directed learning, which is the key to fulfilling your academic goals and your larger life ambitions.

Now, I would like to share with you the story of a young man who overcame all odds to make his dreams come true.

Charles's Story

We begin Charles's story at the low point of his academic career. As a math major from rural Louisiana, Charles had flunked out of LSU not once but twice. After he left school for the second time, Charles decided to volunteer as a football coaching assistant at a prestigious private middle school. An affluent businessman whose son played on the team noticed Charles's infectious optimism and unique brand of compassionate rigor. He also noticed Charles's uncommon rapport with the kids and how effectively he motivated them, so he hired Charles to tutor his son in math. As a result of Charles's tutoring, the businessman's son began to make As. When word got around that the coach's helper was an excellent math tutor, many more parents hired him to tutor their children. The children went from making Cs to As to enjoying math.

The businessman thought to himself, "This guy's too smart not to have a degree." So he contacted a retired LSU administrator to see if he knew anyone who could get Charles readmitted to LSU. He promised that if LSU readmitted Charles, he would pay for everything—tuition, fees, books, meals, and housing. Keep in mind that LSU almost never readmits students who have been dismissed twice for academic reasons. This retired administrator called me and told me about the businessman's offer. He also told me that Charles had graduated from high school with a great GPA and had good standardized test scores but had bombed twice at LSU. I was intrigued and decided to meet with Charles.

During our meeting, I learned that Charles's father had been diagnosed with lung cancer during Charles's fifth year in school. He had bounced from major to major during those five years and hadn't done well academically. After his father's diagnosis, he had spent every weekend driving eight hours round trip to be with his father, who died during the second semester of that year. He was so devastated that he stopped attending classes and was dismissed for academic reasons. After sitting out for a year, he was readmitted. The second time around, Charles began taking more difficult math classes and attempted to do well in those courses on his own, without any assistance from anyone. Although he was encouraged to visit the campus learning center, he resisted because he thought that he should be able to excel in his courses without help. He told me that on one occasion, he even came to the learning center and stood in front of the door but couldn't make himself go in. Over the years I have learned that it is not uncommon for students to get to the door of the campus academic support center and then turn around before going in. But often those who do finally go in say, "I wish I had come sooner!" When I ask them why they didn't come sooner, a typical answer is, "I didn't know this is what you were gonna tell me. I thought you were just gonna tell me to study harder, or spend more time on my studies, or stop socializing so much." Students think they're going to hear things they already know they should be doing, and they have no idea that they will leave the center with powerful learning strategies they can use for their entire academic experience. Tragically, so many students and faculty do not know the immediate and dramatic impact that learning strategies can have. For Charles, that ignorance resulted in his flunking out of school a second time.

After I found out that Charles was willing to implement effective learning strategies, I called the director of admissions on his behalf. I told the director that if he admitted him on a provisional basis for the summer term, I would guarantee that Charles would earn a 4.0 GPA. I assured the director that I fully understood that if Charles didn't get a 4.0, he could be dismissed for good. After expressing surprise that

I would guarantee a 4.0, the director agreed to grant Charles a conditional summer-only admission. Charles took nine credit hours of classes that summer and did achieve the 4.0 that earned him readmission to LSU. He graduated from LSU in August 2009 having earned a 3.4 GPA for all his coursework since that critical summer session. Charles is now living his dream of teaching mathematics to high school and middle school students. He also continues to coach football.

The Sky Is the Limit!

My wish for you is that you, like Charles, see your wildest dreams come true using the power of metacognition. Go forth and prosper.

A Final Activity for You

1. Review the commitment exercise you completed in this chapter. Add more specifics to your commitment. When will you try the strategy or strategies you chose? For what class or classes will you use them?

APPENDIX A

Compilation of Strategies for Students

The 35 strategies listed here are a combination of the metacognitive, learning, study, and testing strategies presented in this book.

1. Strive for higher levels of Bloom's Taxonomy. (Chapter 4)
2. Implement the study cycle and schedule three to four intense study sessions per day. (Chapter 4)
3. Actively prepare to read by previewing reading assignments. (Chapter 5)
4. Read actively by developing questions before you start to read. (Chapter 5)
5. Paraphrase information in each paragraph of a reading assignment. (Chapter 5)
6. Actively read and learn by using flashcards, concept maps, mind maps, and other tools. (Chapter 5, Appendix F)
7. Read the textbook. (Chapter 5)
8. Always attend every class. (Chapter 5)
9. Take good class notes by hand. (Chapter 5)
10. Preview and review for every class. (Chapter 4)
11. Do homework assignments without using examples or textbook information. (Chapter 5)

12. Prepare as if you have to teach the information you are learning. (Chapter 5)
13. Study with a partner or study group, and go to each session prepared. (Chapter 5)
14. Create practice exams to evaluate your mastery of the material. (Chapter 5)
15. Start homework the day that it is assigned and do a little of it each day. (Chapter 9)
16. Adopt a growth mindset about intelligence. (Chapter 6)
17. Monitor your self-talk and stay positive. (Chapter 6)
18. Attribute results to actions, not ability. (Chapter 6)
19. Get adequate rest, nutrition, and exercise. (Chapter 8)
20. Keep a semester calendar. (Chapter 9)
21. Keep a weekly calendar. (Chapter 9)
22. Commit to studying 20 to 25 hours per week. (Chapter 9)
23. Protect your free time. (Chapter 9)
24. Prioritize according to needs and wants. (Chapter 9)
25. Organize test information by preparing charts, outlines, or a study guide. (Chapter 9)
26. Determine the types of questions that upcoming tests will feature (essay, short answer, multiple choice, T/F, etc.). (Chapter 9)
27. Write down formulas or other information you may need before you begin an exam. (Chapter 9)
28. Read test directions *very* carefully, listen for additional directions, and ask for clarification. (Chapter 9)
29. Survey the exam before starting and budget your time. (Chapter 9)
30. Begin with the easiest test questions and work your way up to the harder ones. (Chapter 9)
31. Expect memory blocks and recognize that the information will come back to you if you move on to other questions. (Chapter 9)
32. Perform deep breathing to relax, and use positive self-talk to reduce test anxiety. (Chapter 9)

33. Analyze all returned tests and quizzes, and develop a plan for improvement. (Chapter 9)
34. Use the campus learning center for group study, tutoring, and other helpful information. (Chapter 9)
35. Visit your professors' office hours on a regular basis. (Chapter 7)

APPENDIX B

Books and Links Recommended for Students

- David Ellis. (2014). *Becoming a master student.* Boston, MA: Cengage Learning.
- John Medina. (2008). *Brain rules.* Seattle, WA: Pear Press.
- Carol Dweck. (2006). *Mindset: The new psychology of success.* New York, NY: Random House.
- Terry Doyle and Todd Zakrajsek. (2013). *The new science of learning: How to learn in harmony with your brain.* Sterling, VA: Stylus.
- John N. Gardner and Betsy O. Barefoot. (2016). *Your college experience: Strategies for success* (12th ed.). Boston, MA: Macmillan.

To assess your mindset:
www.mindsetonline.com
For more test-preparation strategies:
www.howtostudy.org
For more learning, study, and testing strategies:
www.lsu.edu/students/cas/
www.drearlbloch.com
For relaxation techniques and stress relief:
www.ucdmc.ucdavis.edu/hr/hrdepts/asap/Documents/
Relaxation_Techniques.pdf

APPENDIX C

Learning Strategies Inventory

This inventory lists behaviors that you should exhibit in order to excel in this course. Write "true" or "false" beside each of the following statements describing the way you study. The scoring scale at the end will predict your grade in the course.

1. I always preview the material that will be discussed before I go to class.
2. I go over my lecture notes as soon as possible after lecture to rework them and note problem areas.
3. I try to do my homework without using example problems as a guide or copying answers from my class notes or textbook.
4. I regularly go to office hours or tutoring to discuss problems or questions about the homework.
5. I rework all of the homework problems and questions before the test or quiz.
6. I spend some time studying for this class at least five days per week (outside of class).
7. I make mnemonics for myself to help me remember facts and equations.
8. I make diagrams or draw mental pictures of the concepts discussed in class.

9. I participate in a study group where we do homework and quiz ourselves on the material.
10. I rework all of the quiz and test items I have missed *before* the next class session.
11. I realize that I can still do well in this class even if I have done poorly on the quizzes and tests up to this point.

The predicted grade for your performance in this class is provided as follows:

Number of True Responses	Predicted Grade
9 or more	A
6–8	B
4–5	C
2–3	D
less than 2	F

Note that you can change your predicted grade at any point by changing your behavior such that more of the statements are true.

APPENDIX D

Dramatic Individual Student Improvement

The following examples are of students whose performance increased dramatically after learning about metacognition, Bloom's Taxonomy, and the study cycle. The students were in classes at different institutions and from different disciplines. All are from semesters between fall 2005 and spring 2014. Underlined scores occurred after the intervention. These are just a fraction of the success stories that have crossed my path.

Robert, freshman, general chemistry	42, <u>100, 100, 100</u>
Michael, senior, organic chemistry	30, 28, <u>80, 91</u>
Miriam, freshman, calculus	37.5, <u>83, 93</u>
Ifeanyi, sophomore, thermodynamics	67, 54, 68, <u>95</u>
Jazmin, freshman, history	44, <u>87, 86</u>
Kristy, freshman, general chemistry	60, <u>100, 99, 84</u>
Adam, senior, analytical chemistry	76, 61, 61, <u>107</u>
Blanche, freshman, general chemistry	63, 79, 87, <u>100</u>
Aaron, freshman, general biology	78, <u>92</u>
Maryan, freshman, art history	57, <u>87</u>
Jessie, freshman, general chemistry	60, <u>92, 83, 83</u>
Frederick, sophomore, analytical chemistry	77, 65, 68, <u>88</u>
Cathy, freshman, trigonometry	77, <u>99</u>
Natalie, freshman, general chemistry	63, 92, 79, <u>96</u>
Elizabeth, freshman, general chemistry	67, <u>84, 87, 87</u>

Stephanie, sophomore, analytical chemistry	83, 55, 65, <u>90</u>
Rachel, freshman, general chemistry	70, <u>92, 95, 84</u>
Morayo, sophomore, organic chemistry	61, 73, <u>99</u>
Cory, freshman, psychology	68, <u>83, 82, 86, 82</u>
Miranda, freshman, psychology	65, <u>84, 86, 88, 82</u>
M'Famara, sophomore, analytical chemistry	70, 46, 68, <u>88</u>
Matt, freshman, general chemistry	65, 55, <u>95</u>

APPENDIX E

Selected Student Feedback

I decided to include this somewhat arbitrary selection of student feedback so that readers might have a visceral experience of the relief and excitement some students feel when they are introduced to metacognition and learning strategies. The content of student correspondence has been faithfully reproduced; spelling and grammar have been largely but not completely standardized.

From Matt J., Weber State University, Class of 2016
September 15, 2014

Dr. McGuire,
My name is Matt, I am a junior at Weber State. I was present on Thursday for your presentation on metacognition. Before I share the effect it is already having I would like to tell you about myself. I am a high school dropout, "class" of 06, I started college in 2011. I am 26, married with 2 kids ages 2 and 6 months. . . . With a truly incredible amount of things that need my attention every day, I really must make the most of my class time, and also my study time. Suffering toward the severe side of ADD, it is a task itself to stay focused, let alone deep focus. Honestly it can be so frustrating trying to learn or study and just not have the ability to focus my thoughts. I feel at times I am just not smart enough to keep up with college and should just quit. It is even a bit emotional as I think about the future for my family. I am not a quitter though. Now the exciting part! I have tried the suggestions you gave in your presentation, and it was like magic, seriously. When I was studying my chemistry this past week, even if I have to reference

my outline multiple times to stay on track, organizing my information differently somehow has made what I was studying at the time stick so much better. I think probably because my brain knew where to put the information??? I hope to master these techniques and share them with everyone. My plan is to increase my GPA so I can get into grad school. I want to say thank you, because not only do I feel I am learning more efficiently and I feel like my self-esteem is going up, but it is also allowing me the much needed little bit of extra time to spend with my wife and kids because I am understanding concepts quicker and better. Thank you again so much. These methods are changing my life. . . .

Best regards,
Matt J.

September 30, 2014

Dr. Mac,
I had my first test in principles of chemistry (II) this past weekend. Let's just say . . . I could not have dreamed of it going any better! My first two quizzes I failed, and my first lab report I did very poorly also. Luckily they are not worth many points. I definitely feel like I tripped straight out of the gate and fell flat on my face in this class. Now it is totally going up! My homework scores are progressively going up. I aced my last two quizzes and as far as my test I got an 85%! The reason I am so excited about that is, there were two questions that I knew I had not gone over enough to build the connections and reason my way through them, so I worked them the best I could. A third question I felt like I was 70% there with what I needed to know but at a crucial point just could not get past where I needed to and nearly ran out of time. What was so exciting was I was so confident in my answers because of the way I had organized the information in my head and how given the information I was able to solve the problem. I knew almost instantly what formulas would apply, what exceptions needed to be taken into consideration, and so on. I really am starting to see things increase greatly in this class, and I know it will continue to get even better for me! I have realized also, now being in a position to help/explain concepts, that if

I follow some of these metacognition methods it is so easy to clarify to other students. Then they go ("Oh!" Well ok, that is simple enough). It's simple because they are looking at the problem now in a much more efficient way of understanding!

—Matt J.

From Sydnie L., LSU, Class of 2017
January 20, 2014

Hi Dr. McGuire,
This is Sydnie L., the student you talked with after giving the CAS presentation to Dr. Cook's Honors Chem 1421 class. I just wanted to thank you for giving me the tools I needed to succeed in my classes. . . . For Chem 1421, I made sure to preview the textbook and note templates before class. I took detailed notes so that I wouldn't be confused by my gibberish later when studying. I tried to review my notes shortly after chemistry lecture, and to work homework problems while the information was still fresh. I studied hard before each exam. I would work as many practice problems as I could, and if I wasn't sure how to work a problem I would visit the tutors in the Tutorial Center. I made sure to work almost all of the recommended practice problems for the end of each chapter (I really think this was the most helpful change I made). I attended as many [supplemental instruction] sessions as time allowed. I also took advantage of every bonus assignment, not only for the points but also as a learning opportunity.

Sincerely,
Sydnie L.

May 7, 2014

Hey Dr. McGuire!
I'm so sorry that it has been so long since we have talked. This semester has been much more busy for me than last semester. I was much more active with LSU Ambassadors as well as my part-time job at a

dermatology office. I also spent a great deal of time training to be an orientation leader for LSU this summer. You'll be pleased to hear that I expect to finish the semester with a 4.0 again! I made it my goal to work hard early in the semester, and maintain high averages in all of my courses. Toward the end of the semester things got crazy and I didn't study as hard, and my exams showed that. I didn't do well on Dr. Cook's final, but I earned the grade I received because I didn't study the way I should have. But because I worked hard early in the semester, I'll still pull a low A in Chem 1422. I'll be sure to use this exam as a reminder of why it's so important to stay dedicated to my study strategies all semester long, and will work much harder next semester. . . . All things considered, I'm still proud of myself and the grades that I have made this semester.

Sincerely,
Sydnie L.

From Morgan B., Nursing Major, Lynchburg College, Class of 2017
February 3, 2014

I just wanted to thank you for coming to Lynchburg College and sharing your strategies with us. I have been practicing your studying recommendations and I just took a quiz in bio today and got a 100%! I find it extremely helpful and it should make nursing school easier on me. Thank you so much!

—Morgan B.

From Anetra Grice, Western Michigan University Program Director, Feedback From Two Students
February 19, 2013

Hi Saundra!
I wanted to pass along a few student comments we've received from recent meetings we've held as part of our early intervention project. These comments directly reference the benefits of sitting down with

students and explaining the learning cycle. I thought you might enjoy hearing how your visit with us has directly impacted our students!

My biggest problem last semester was sitting down and taking the time to study and evaluate the course material, for tests or homework, which hurt me the most! I spent maybe 3 hours or less a week on studying or doing homework. This semester I have made a MAJOR change in my study habits! Instead of hanging out with friends right after class, I now spend at least 30 minutes reviewing my class notes and digesting the lecture. I stopped going home on weekends, because I wasn't doing my homework or studying there. I now dedicate my Saturday and Sunday morning to studying and homework. While this is not an overnight fix I believe I'm taking a step in the right direction. The meeting with Bryan was helpful in the fact that it made me realize that I'm no longer in High School and that the study routine which worked for me there will NOT work here. I respect and VERY much appreciate the meeting. It's very nice knowing I go to a school where the faculty truly look out for your best interest and want you to succeed!! I very much look forward to follow-up emails with you and any suggestion, ideas, or constructive criticism you have for me that will help me benefit in my studies here at WMU!

Yes I found the meeting to be extremely helpful. I have been following his advice on documenting my study times. I have not made it to 30 hours each week, but I am steadily increasing my study hours each week to reach the goal. Please give Dr. Tsang my thanks. What he showed me has been wonderful. On both of my exams so far this semester I passed them with flying colors and on one of the exams I got the highest grade in the class.

Thank you again for your help and I hope that you are well!

Anetra Grice
WMU-STEP Program Director
College of Engineering and Applied Sciences, Western Michigan University

From Ben M., Mathematics Major, University of Mississippi
September 4, 2012

My name is Ben. I am a math undergraduate at Ole Miss. We met over the summer at a mentor workshop during the SMILE program at LSU. I just wanted to write and say thank you for the work that you have done. I have used a lot of the things that you presented to us during your workshop. And I only started this summer, but they are really helping me this semester.

I was the outstanding math student at Northwest Mississippi Community College when I graduated in 2008 and then I was out of school for 3 years. When I returned to school last fall I had a lot of trouble concentrating, procrastinating, and I did not do well at all. In the spring semester things were even worse. After two semesters my GPA went from a 3.97 to a 3.11. I thought I might not be able to finish a degree.

This semester I am armed with the resources and knowledge that you provided to us in your workshop, and without them I don't think I would have come back this fall, or been prepared when I did. I know I have not finished the story here, but if you had to wait till the end to know you made a difference, well, that just wouldn't be any fun at all. Thanks again,
Ben

From a Student of Chemistry Instructor Catherine Situma, Louisiana State University
June 25, 2009

I have always had a difficult time understanding Chemistry—even in high school. But I have always made good grades. Well, last fall I did not do well in Chemistry 1201 at all. I did not understand why I did so badly. Anyway I had to retake the class this semester and I failed the first test the second time around in Chem 1201! Thank you Dr. Situma for inviting the wonderful Dr. Saundra McGuire to teach us how to study general chemistry!! I had spoken with Dr. McGuire once before and she explained many of the situations to me like she did that day in class. Having met her and seeing her again that day made me realize I had been studying for Chem 1201 all wrong. Now I know that I cannot study for Chemistry the way I do in other classes. She made me understand that. I especially liked the idea of preview-review. That really helped me pass this class this semester—I got a B in Chem 1201 after flunking it last semester!!! I am very content with the B. Thanks again, Dr. Situma.

From a Student of History Instructor Carla Falkner, Northeast Mississippi Community College
February 8, 2007

Thanks. Metacognition made a BIG difference in my grade. I found out that I am an auditory learner—recording the lectures works best for me. I realized that a lot of words are flying over my head while I am taking notes, key pieces that can help me to produce a clearer image. Some of my notes were taken so quickly that I couldn't make ANY sense out of them when I tried to read them, but now I have a tape to back them up so I can figure out what they were supposed to mean. I just thought you would like some positive feedback since you keep taking the time to inform us with metacognition. I cannot say the word hardly or spell it but without a doubt I know it WORKS!!!!

From Candace E., Southern University of New Orleans Chemistry Student
I wanted to say thank you for helping me improve my study skills in Chemistry. When I met you I was repeating General Chemistry for the second time, failed three tests, and I had an "F" average for midterms. I never understood how I could study for hours and still fail my chemistry tests. Then I went on LSU's Center for Academic Success website and realized that I was studying wrong. So with your help I'm no longer intimidated by chemistry or any other subject for that matter. This semester my goal is to make As in General Chemistry 112 and 112 Lab. Today is the first day of school for Southern University at New Orleans and I went to my chemistry class ready

to discuss Chapter 15. My Professor, Dr. Bopp, asked ME to slow down. I told him you can't slow down when you're on a roll!!!!!!!!!!

—Candace E.

From a Student of Chemistry Instructor Algernon Kelley, The College at Brockport, SUNY
May 28, 2015

Dear Dr. Kelley,
First of all, I wanted to thank you very sincerely for taking the time early in the spring semester to come talk to our biochem 2 class. In addition, I cannot thank you enough for meeting with me to talk about how to adjust my own study strategies and improve my scholastic performance at the beginning of the semester.

When you came to our biochem class to talk about improving study habits, I hadn't done terribly on the first biochem exam—I just hadn't done as well as I would have liked. However, I was very worried about my present ineffective study strategies for physics 240 with Dr. Tahar. I also was hoping to improve my biochem 2 grade. You gave me some of the best advice I have received in my three years of undergrad. You told me to start (1) working out homework problems without the Internet on paper, (2) going to every class, (3) reviewing what would be taught in class, (4) getting help from the professor as a last resort when I couldn't figure out a problem, rather than turning to the Internet, and finally (5) keeping my phone off as much as possible and not listening to music as I work. After hearing all this, I will be honest and say I really didn't think it would work for me. I thought that physics 235 with Dr. Tahar had been impossibly difficult and physics 240 would be equally, if not more so, difficult. I had been attending class before talking to you but had been texting and not paying attention during class thinking "there's no way I will understand anyway." However, after talking to you, I decided to try some of the strategies. I started working out 1–3 homework problems before class in a quiet room during my 1-hour break between classes. I also reviewed the chapter before going to class. I started keeping my phone off except for certain times, like lunch or when I had to meet up with someone. The results were surprisingly drastic. The next exam after talking to you I got over 20 points higher than the class average. I was so excited and couldn't wait to tell you. However, I decided to continue studying in addition to the few things I had already tried that you advised me to do. I decided to also try to do as many odd-numbered end of chapter problems as possible to help prepare me for the next test. The last thing I wanted was to do worse on the next exam. Again, I improved from the last test.

For your future talks in front of freshman, sophomore, junior, or even senior audiences, my grades can be an example of how heeding your excellent suggestions can transform grades.

Biochem 2: spring 2015—(there was a fourth exam but I never was able to see what I got on the take-home portion, which was 50% of the grade, so I left that grade out)

- Exam 1: 84% (without your study strategies)
- Exam 2: 87%
- Exam 3: 90%
- ACS Final Exam: 47/60 (this grade was in the 87th percentile nationally)

Final grade in class: A−

Physics 235 with Dr. Tahar: fall 2014—(without your study strategies)

- Exam 1: 66%
- Exam 2: 52%
- Exam 3: 36%
- Exam 4: not sure what this grade was

Lab grade: 97%
Homework: 100% (thank you Internet)
Rocket launch: extra 2% toward final grade
Final grade in class: C+

Physics 240 with Dr. Tahar: spring 2015—(with your study strategies for Exams 2–4)

- Exam 1: 71% (without your study strategies)
- Exam 2: 83%
- Exam 3: 86%
- Exam 4: 91%

Lab grade: 98%
Homework: 100% (doing problems with the help of my book and professor when necessary for the most part)
Rocket launch: extra 2% toward final grade in class
Final grade in class: A

Thank you for giving me such great advice and for following up on me throughout the semester.

Thanks!
Sincerely,
Autumn

APPENDIX F

Study Tools

The tools listed here, in no particular order, are options for you to use during the second stage of an intense study session when you engage in active learning tasks. Because each learner is highly individual, you should experiment until you find what works for you. If you have a system that works and does not include a single tool on this list, that is perfectly fine. Whatever floats your boat. If you want even more suggestions for study tools, visit your campus learning center and speak to the professionals there.

One more thing: Many websites and apps are mentioned in this list as examples, but I am not endorsing or recommending any particular tool. If an alternative works better for you, please use it. Moreover, if you find that going old school and doing everything analog and by hand works best for you, please do that! The research supporting my recommendation to take class notes by hand may well be valid for other learning activities.

1. **Flashcards**
   This tool is perfect for classes requiring lots of memorization. You can create flashcards by hand, or you can use online tools like memorize.com or Quizlet.

2. **Highlighting**
   Highlighter pens of different colors can be used to efficiently organize information. For example, a U.S. History student learning about the Civil War might highlight all

Union politicians and military officials in blue while using a different color for those affiliated with the Confederacy. You can highlight assigned reading, lecture notes posted by instructors, your own notes, returned tests and quizzes, and anything else that is helpful. (Do not highlight any material you plan to subsequently sell or rent.)

3. **Mnemonic Devices**

   A mnemonic device is anything that can be used as a memory aid, including acronyms (ROYGBIV for the color spectrum), short poems (i before e except after c), phrases to help remember first letters of words (My Very Educated Mother Just Served Us Nachos for planetary names), or visual devices (right-hand rule for the orthogonality of magnetic and electric fields).

4. **Timers**

   You can use your smartphone timer or an app like the popular Marinara Timer to keep from feeling overwhelmed and to ensure that you get enough breaks. (If you can't face a 40-minute intense study session at the end of long day, you could still try 5 or 10 minutes, right?)

5. **Note Taking**

   You can take notes in class, while reading the textbook, while perusing multimedia supplemental materials, or even from existing notes. How to take notes is a highly individual question. If you don't have your system quite figured out yet, check out the Cornell Note Taking System and Evernote. Your Internet search engine can tell you more. And don't forget that you can record lectures and take notes from the recordings.

6. **Mapping**

   Visual, nonlinear organization of information is often very helpful. There are an infinite number of ways to do it. You may have heard of mind mapping, concept mapping, or chapter mapping, just three types of this very versatile tool. Flowcharts are also a popular kind of mapping. Again, experimentation and flexibility are key. There is no right or wrong way to map. Use your Internet search engine to check out your options and decide what works for you. If you want to use an online tool, there are many websites and apps that can assist you in mapping.

7. Study Guides: Outlines and Charting
One popular way of studying for an exam is to create a study guide for a unit or group of units. That way, especially if the course is cumulative, you have a handy reference for review later in the semester or year. Two useful ways (but certainly not the only ways) to organize information in a study guide are outlining and charting. First, you probably learned to outline in middle school or high school, using Roman numerals (I, II, III) for the highest level of organization, then capital letters (A, B, C) for the next-highest level, then numbers (1, 2, 3), and so on. The information presented in a textbook should follow a clear outline that you can deduce, for example. Second, charting—whereby information is organized into rows and columns—can be especially useful for organizing historical events or systems of scientific classification. Outlines and charting can also be used as stand-alone tools, not in the context of a study guide.

8. Testing Apps and Software
Creating a practice quiz or test by hand has much to recommend it. But if you prefer to go a digital route, there is a plethora of quiz-making software out there, including memorize.com and Quizlet.

For more suggestions and ideas, visit your campus learning center.

REFERENCES

Adams, R., & Biddle, B. (1970). The classroom scene. *Realities of teaching.* New York, NY: Holt, Rinehart, & Winston.

Aguilar, L., Walton, G., & Wieman, C. (2014). Psychological insights for improved physics teaching. *Physics Today, 67,* 43–49.

Ambrose, S. A., Bridges, M. W., DiPietro, M., Lovett, M. C., & Norman, M. K. (2010). *How learning works: Seven research-based principles for smart teaching.* San Francisco, CA: Jossey-Bass.

Anderson, L. W., Krathwohl, D. R., Airasian, P. W., Cruikshank, K. A., Mayer, R. E., Pintrich, P. R., . . . Wittrock, M. C. (2001). *A taxonomy of learning, teaching, and assessing: A revision of Bloom's taxonomy of educational objectives.* New York, NY: Longman.

Bloom, B. S., Englehart, M. B., Furst, E. J., Hill, W. H., & Krathwohl, D. R. (1956). *Taxonomy of educational objectives: The classification of educational goals* (Vol. 1). New York, NY: McKay.

Bunce, D., Komperda, R., Schroeder, M. J., Dillner, D. K., Lin, S., Teichert, M. A., & Hartmann, J. R. (in press). Differential use of study approaches by students of different achievement levels. *Journal of Chemical Education.*

Bransford, J. (1979). *Human cognition: Learning, understanding, and remembering.* Belmont, CA: Wadsworth.

Brown, P. C., Roediger, H. L., III, & McDaniel, M. A. (2014). *Make it stick: The science of successful learning.* Cambridge, MA: Harvard University Press.

Bruner, J. (1985). Vygotsky: An historical and conceptual perspective. In J. V. Wertsch (Ed.), *Culture, communication, and cognition: Vygotskian perspectives* (pp. 21–34). London, UK: Cambridge University Press.

Carey, B. (2010, September 6). Forget what you know about good study habits. *New York Times.* Retrieved from http://www.nytimes.com/2010/09/07/health/views/07mind.html

Carey, B. (2014, November 22). Studying for the test by taking it. *New York Times*. Retrieved from http://www.nytimes.com/2014/11/23/sunday-review/studying-for-the-test-by-taking-it.html

Christ, F. L. (1997). *Seven steps to better management of your study time*. Clearwater, FL: H & H Publishing.

Cook, E., Kennedy, E., & McGuire, S. Y. (2013). Effect of teaching metacognitive learning strategies on performance in general chemistry courses. *Journal of Chemical Education, 90,* 961–967.

Dewar, M., Alber, J., Butler, C., Cowan, N., & Della Sala, S. (2012). Brief wakeful resting boosts new memories over the long term. *Psychological Science, 23*(9), 955–960.

Doyle, T., & Zakrajsek, T. (2013). *The new science of learning: How to learn in harmony with your brain*. Sterling, VA: Stylus.

Dunlosky, J. (2013). Strengthening the student toolbox: Study strategies to boost learning. *American Educator*. Retrieved from https://www.aft.org/sites/default/fi les/periodicals/dunlosky.pdf

Dweck, C. S. (2006). *Mindset: The new psychology of success*. New York, NY: Random House.

Eagan, M. K., Stolzenberg, E. B., Zimmerman, H. B., Aragon, M. C., Whang Sayson, H., & Rios-Aguilar, C. (2017). *The American freshman: National norms fall 2016*. Los Angeles, CA: Higher Education Research Institute, UCLA.

Ellis, D. (2014). *Becoming a master student*. Boston, MA: Cengage Learning.

Flavell, J. H. (1976). Metacognitive aspects of problem solving. In L. B. Resnick (Ed.), *The nature of intelligence* (pp. 231–236). Hillsdale, NJ: Erlbaum.

Gardner, J. N., & Barefoot, B. O. (2016). *Your college experience: Strategies for success* (12th ed.). Boston, MA: Macmillan.

Gardner, J. N., Jewler, A. J., & Barefoot, B. O. (2009). *Your college experience: Strategies for success* (8th ed.). Boston, MA: Wadsworth Cengage Learning.

Gregory, G., & Parry, T. (2006). *Designing brain-compatible learning*. Thousand Oaks, CA: Corwin Press.

Hirsch, G. (2001). *Helping college students succeed: A model for effective intervention*. Philadelphia, PA: Brunner-Routledge.

Hobson, E. (2001). *Motivating students to learn in large classes*. Unpublished manuscript, Albany College of Pharmacy, Albany, NY.

Hoffman, R., & McGuire, S. Y. (2010). Learning and teaching strategies. *American Scientist, 98,* 378–382.

Hopper, C. H. (2013). *Practicing college learning strategies* (6th ed.). Boston, MA: Wadsworth.

Hunt, A. M. W., & Swogger, J. G. (n.d.) Unlocking the past! Radiocarbon Dating. *Carbon Comics No. 1*, Center for the Applied Isotope Studies, University of Georgia.

Kandel, E. R., Schwartz J. H., Jessell, T. M., Siegelbaum, S. A., & Hudspeth, A. J. (2013). *Principles of neural science* (5th ed.). New York, NY: McGraw-Hill.

Karns, C. M., Dow, M. W., & Neville, H. J. (2012). Altered cross-modal processing in the primary auditory cortex of congenitally deaf adults: A visual-somatosensory fMRI study with a double-flash illusion. *The Journal of Neuroscience, 32*(28), 9626–9638.

Klingner, J., & Vaughn, S. (1999). Promoting reading comprehension, content learning, and English acquisition through collaborative strategic reading (CSR). *The Reading Teacher, 52*(7), 738–747.

Leelawong, K., & Biswas, G. (2008). Designing learning by teaching agents: The Betty's Brain system. *International Journal of Artifi cial Intelligence and Education, 18*(3), 181–208.

McGuire, S. Y. (2015). *Teach students how to learn: Strategies you can incorporate into any course to improve student metacognition, study skills, and motivation.* Sterling, VA: Stylus Publishing.

Medina, J. (2008). *Brain rules.* Seattle, WA: Pear Press.

Mueller, P. A., & Oppenheimer, D. M. (2014). The pen is mightier than the keyboard: Advantages of longhand over laptop note taking. *Psychological Science, 25*(6), 1159–1168.

Nilson, L. (2004). *Teaching at its best: A research-based resource for college instructors.* Bolton, MA: Anker.

Nixon, C. L. (2007, November 2). *Learned helplessness* [Video]. Retrieved from https://www.youtube.com/watch?v=gFmFOmprTt0

Overbaugh, R. (n.d.). *Bloom's Taxonomy.* Norfolk, VA: Old Dominion University.

Overbaugh, R., & Schultz, L. (n.d.). *Image of two versions of Bloom's Taxonomy.* Norfolk, VA: Old Dominion University. Retrieved from www.odu.edu/educ/roverbau/Bloom/blooms_taxonomy.htm

Pennebaker, J. W., Gosling, S. D., & Ferrell, J. D. (2013). Daily online testing in large classes: Boosting college performance while reducing achievement gaps. *PLoS ONE, 8*(11). doi:10.1371/journal.pone.0079774

Roediger, H. L., III, & Karpicke, J. D. (2006). Test-enhanced learning. *Psychological Science, 17*(3), 249–255.

Seligman, M. E. P., & Maier, S. F. (1967). Failure to escape traumatic shock. *Journal of Experimental Psychology, 74*, 1–9.

Shenk, D. (2010). *The genius in all of us: Why everything you've been told about genetics, talent, and IQ is wrong.* New York, NY: Doubleday.

Staley, C. (2007). *Focus on college and career success.* Boston, MA: Cengage Learning.

Stevenson, H. W., & Stigler, J. W. (1992). *The learning gap: Why our schools are failing and what we can learn from Japanese and Chinese education.* New York, NY: Summit Books.

Talanquer, V., & Pollard, J. (2010). Let's teach how we think instead of what we know. *Chemical Education Research and Practice, 11*(2), 74–83.

Uttal, D. H. (1997). Beliefs about genetic influences on mathematics achievement: A cross-cultural comparison. *Genetica, 99,* 165–172.

Vygotsky, L. (1978). *Mind in society: The development of higher psychological processes.* Cambridge, MA: Harvard University Press.

Yeager, D. S., Garcia, J., Brzustoski, P., Hessert, W. T., Purdie-Vaughns, V., Apfel, N., . . . Cohen, G. L. (2013). Breaking the cycle of mistrust: Wise interventions to provide critical feedback across the racial divide. *Journal of Experimental Psychology: General, 143*(2), 804–824.

Zhao, N., Wardeska, J. G., McGuire, S. Y., & Cook, E. (2014). Metacognition: An effective tool to promote success in college science learning. *Journal of College Science Teaching, 43*(4), 48–54.

Zull, J. E. (2011). *From brain to mind: Using neuroscience to guide change in education.* Sterling, VA: Stylus.

ABOUT THE AUTHORS

Saundra Yancy McGuire

Saundra Yancy McGuire is director emerita of the nationally acclaimed Center for Academic Success and a retired assistant vice chancellor and professor of chemistry at Louisiana State University. She received the Presidential Award for Excellence in Science, Mathematics, and Engineering Mentoring in a White House Oval Office Ceremony, and in 2017 she was inducted into the Louisiana State University (LSU) College of Science Hall of Distinction. She is an elected fellow of the American Association for the Advancement of Science, the American Chemical Society, and the Council of Learning Assistance and Developmental Education Associations. Additionally, she is a recipient of the College Reading and Learning Association Distinguished Teaching Award and has achieved Level Four Lifetime Learning Center Leadership Certification through the National College Learning Center Association. Prior to joining LSU in August 1999, she spent 11 years at Cornell University, where she received the coveted Clark Distinguished Teaching Award.

Dr. McGuire has been teaching and mentoring students for over forty-five years and conducting faculty development workshops for over three decades. She has delivered keynote addresses or presented student and faculty development workshops at over 300 institutions in 45 states and 9 countries. Her work has been published in *Science, The Journal of Chemical Education, American Scientist, The Learning Assistance Review, To Improve the Academy,* and *New Directions for Teaching and Learning.*

Dr. McGuire received her bachelor's degree, magna cum laude, from Southern University in Baton Rouge, Louisiana; her master's degree from Cornell University; and her doctoral degree from the University of Tennessee at Knoxville, where she received the Chancellor's Citation for Exceptional Professional Promise. She is married to Dr. Stephen C. McGuire, James and Ruth Smith Endowed Professor of Physics at Southern University. They are the parents of Dr. Carla McGuire Davis and Dr. Stephanie McGuire, and the doting grandparents of Joshua, Ruth, Daniel, and Joseph Davis.

Stephanie McGuire

Stephanie McGuire holds a bachelor's degree in biology from the Massachusetts Institute of Technology, a master's degree and a doctoral degree in neuroscience from the University of Oxford, and a master's degree in opera performance from the Longy Conservatory. She attended Oxford on a Marshall scholarship and received a graduate fellowship from the National Science Foundation. Her doctoral dissertation explores how the human ear and brain process broadband, 20-microsecond clicks. At the Longy Conservatory, she received the Victor Rosenbaum medal, given yearly to the most outstanding graduate of the conservatory.

Partly as a result of long and stimulating conversations with her mother about pedagogy and learning strategies, she became a highly sought-after private academic tutor in the New York City area where she lived for 10 years. By coauthoring this book, she is delighted to contribute to Dr. Saundra McGuire's admirable and revolutionary mission to make all students expert learners.

Since graduating from conservatory, she has enjoyed forging a successful career as a classical mezzo-soprano. She has performed with the New York City Opera at Lincoln Center, with the Boston Pops Orchestra in Symphony Hall, and several times at Carnegie Hall. She now lives in Berlin, Germany. Please visit www.mcguiremezzo.com to discover more and learn about her upcoming performances.

academic performance, 1, 5, 17
America *versus* Asia on, 61–63
learning strategies improving, 9
student control of, 21
active learning, 71
behavior resulting in, 84
mental processing controlled by,
10
metacognition as, 20
sequential courses for, 87–88
in study sessions, 35, 37
success attributed to, 83–84
America *versus* Asia, 61–63
analysis
Bloom's Taxonomy including, 23,
30, 31
Goldilocks habits as, 32
of mistakes after exams, 98
Anderson, Lorin, 29–30
assessment
in Bloom's Taxonomy, 24
learning and homework as, 54
as questions in notes, 46
study cycle as, 35
teach mode as, 54

Ball, Pam, 25
behavior
active learning as, 84

growth mindset changing, 67
Betty's Brain, ix
Bloom, Benjamin, 30
Bloom's Taxonomy, 21, 38n1
Anderson update on, 29–30
Bloom original of, 30
comprehension in, 29–30, 34
concept application from, 23, 30,
31
details of, 29–38
as four-step process, 23–34
Goldilocks and, 32–33
hierarchy of learning levels as, 23
knowledge *versus* information
from, 38n1
Krathwohl update on, 29–30
reflective questions of, 24
as remembering, understanding,
applying, analyzing, evaluating,
creating, 23, 30, 31
self-assessment in, 24
shallow to deep learning with, 23
studying *versus* learning in,
24–27
brain training
Betty's Brain as, ix
good nutrition for, 85
homework for, 53
mindset changing for, 69–70

Carey, Benedict, 55–56
Center for Academic Success at
  LSU, 2
centers for learning
  employment at, 99
  for learning strategies, 103
  tutoring at, 99
Charles
  as flunked math major, 102
  learning centers not used by, 103
  mathematics teacher as, 104
charting, 125
Christ, F. L., 35
class attendance
  college information from, 35–36
  for note taking, 50–51, 124
  questions asked in, 36
  study cycle as, 35
  T Zone seating in, 50–51
classes
  learning strategies for different,
    101
  preview reading as before, 109
  quiz reviews before, 110
  weekly calendar for, 92
class notes. *See* notes
class participation, 36
college, 7–8
  Bloom's Taxonomy in, 34
  class attendance with information
    in, 35–36
comprehension
  active reading increasing, x
  in Bloom's Taxonomy, 29–30, 34
  tests as increasing, 55
computer program
  Betty's Brain as, ix
  Evernote as, 124
  mapping online tools as, 125

Marinara Timer app as, 124
memorize.com as, 123, 125
  Quizlet online tool as, 123, 125
concept application, 10
  Bloom's Taxonomy as, 23, 30, 31
  diagrams and mental pictures for,
    109
  Goldilocks predicted as, 32
  learning as long-term, 19, 25
  learning strategies for, 67
  mapping as, 101, 124–25
  problem solving from, 31
Cornell Note Taking System, 124
Cornell University, 3–5, 124
creating
  Bloom's Taxonomy as, 31
  Goldilocks extrapolated as, 32–33
  student and environment from,
    83
criticism, 63

Dana
  homework testing knowledge of,
    51
  metacognition for, 13
divide and conquer strategy, 58n1
Dweck, Carol, 59, 83

effort, America *versus* Asia on, 61–63
environment
  faculty and sink or swim, 76–77
  learning supported in, 81
  motivation influenced by, 74
  student creating, 83
evaluating
  Bloom and differences understood
    from, 31
  Goldilocks justified as, 32
Evernote, 124

example problems
 answers compared with solutions
  of, 52
 comprehension and notes with, 46
 homework before checking, 52,
  109
 simple before complex on, 53–54,
  70
 textbooks with, 47
example solutions, 51–52
exams. *See also* quizzes
 easy questions as first in, 98
 homework as preparation for, 96
 information covered in, 97
 mock test and quiz for, 55–56,
  97–98
 note formulas early in, 98
 preparation for, 97–98
 semester calendar schedule for,
  90–91, 97
 stress release techniques in, 98
 syllabus, notes, homework,
  quizzes for, 55
exercise
 deep breathing as, 98
 as scheduled in week, 88
 students without, 75
 success supported by, 85–86

faculty, ix, 1, 36
 emotions influencing, 79
 office hour visits of, 79–80
 respect and knowledge of, 79
 sink or swim environment from,
  76–77
 syllabus for expectations from,
  78–79
 textbooks for knowledge of, 47
 textbooks of, 47, 79

fixed mindset
 American *versus* Asian children
  on, 62
 criticism response of, 63
 gifted students adopting, 64, 65
 growth mindset compared with,
  61
 intellect view resulting in, 59–73
 as kryptonite in school, 60
 labeled children producing, 65
 mistakes as failure for, 62
flashcards
 for memorization, 101, 123
 memorize.com for, 123, 125
 as notes, 46
 Quizlet online tool for, 123, 125
 study sessions with, 37
Flavell, John H., 10, 11
flowcharts, 125

gifted students, 64, 65
goals, 19
Goldilocks, Bloom's Taxonomy and,
 32–33
Goldstein, Mel, 4
grades, 17
 academic success as, 1, 18
 active learning as influencing, 71
 without deep learning, 6, 20
 learning strategies for higher, 2,
  5, 66
 LSI strategies for, 56–57
group learning
 cooperative learning as, ix
 teach mode in, 54–55
growth mindset
 American *versus* Asian children
  on, 62
 criticism response of, 63

easy problems first for, 70
effort over ability for, 71
fate mastered by, 60
fixed mindset compared with, 61
intellect resulting in, 59–73
learned helplessness *versus*, 70
mistakes for, 62
motivation from, 83
success for change to, 68–69

Higher Education Research
    Institute, 6, 7
highlighting
colors for different information,
    123–24
of published material or notes,
    123–24
high school
Bloom's Taxonomy in, 34
college warnings from, 7–8
homework, 8
American *versus* Asian parents on,
    62
as upon assignment, 93
for brain training, 53
class notes and textbook review
    after, 109
example problems and solutions
    of, 51–52, 109
knowledge testing with, 51–54
learning strategies with, 93, 96
mistakes as good in, 53
mock exams from, 55
as nonrequired for learning, 4
reading for, 51–52
as reworked before tests, 109
study buddy for, 110
horizons of learning, 7

ideas, 31, 36
indexes, 49–50
innate ability, America *versus* Asia
    on, 61–63
Institute of Reading Development, 41
intellect
belief influencing, 60
as fixed or growing, 59–73
teaching for development of, 4

Jefferson, Jack, 3
Joshua, 46, 49, 71

knowledge, 19
faculty textbooks for, 47, 79
gifted students as not having, x,
    64, 65
homework as testing, 51–54
information *versus*, 38n1
students and learning, 6–8
Krathwohl, David, 29–30

learned helplessness, 70
learning, 4–5, 9–11, 14, 54, 100.
    See also active learning; learning
    strategies; *specific topics*
Bloom's Taxonomy for, 23
divide and conquer for shallow,
    58n1
emotions influencing, 73–81
environment supportive of, 81
good grades without, 6, 20
habits of, 7–8
as how, why, what if, 25
practice tests for, 19
rereading after problems for, 52
rest following, 37
switching to mode of, 26–27
learning levels

Bloom's Taxonomy as hierarchy of, 23
  of college, 34
learning strategies, x–xi, 9, 20, 100
  classes requiring different, 101
  concept application from, 67
  for higher grades, 2, 5, 66
  homework with, 93, 96
  inventory of, 109–10
  learning centers for, 103
  of metacognition, 40–58
  scientific method for, 101
  smartness depending on, 65–66
  for success, emotions, motivation, 82–83
  teach mode as, 29
Learning Strategies Inventory (LSI), 56–57
logic of discipline, 4
Louisiana State University (LSU), 1, 7, 10
  Center for Academic Success at, 2
  Christ and Center of Academic Success of, 35
LSI. *See* Learning Strategies Inventory
LSU. *See* Louisiana State University

mapping
  charts, graphs, diagrams as, 47
  diagrams and mental pictures as, 109
  as flowcharts and online tools, 125
  as mind, concept, or chapter, 124–25
  as notations, 46
  in study sessions, 37
  as visual, nonlinear organization, 124–25

meanings, 16, 18
memorization
  Bloom's Taxonomy as, 23, 30, 31
  flashcards for, 101, 123
  memorize.com for, 123, 125
  mnemonic devices aid for, 124
  phrases in, 16–17
  as student journey, 3–5
  studying as short-term, 25
  understanding *versus*, 11
mental processing, 10
metacognition, 21n1
  active learning as, 20
  blame to control with, 9–22
  Flavell coining term of, 10–11
  learning differently as, 12
  learning strategies of, 20, 40–58
  paraphrasing in, 40
  study cycle with, 34
  textbooks and strategies of, 49
mind maps, 124–25
  concept application needing, 101
  study sessions with, 37
Mindset, 59
mistakes
  American *versus* Asian children on, 62–63
  in homework as good, 53
mnemonic memory aids
  acronyms, poems, phrases, visuals as, 124
  facts and equations remembered from, 109
motivation
  cycle of, 74
  emotions influencing, 73–81
  faculty obstacles for student, 76–77
  increasing of, 85

learning strategies for, 82–83
self-talk influencing, 83–84
student levers and obstacles for,
    75–76
success and values influencing, 74

Nixon, Charisse L.
    on learned helplessness, 70
    on social psychology, 72n1
notes
    as in class, while studying, from
        notes, 124
    class attendance for taking,
        50–51, 124
    Cornell Note Taking System for,
        124
    Evernote for, 124
    flashcards, mapping, outlines as,
        46
    formulas early in exams as, 98
    highlighting of, 123–24
    mock exams from lecture, 55
    review of, 36, 109
    sample problems, assessment
        questions as, 46
nutrition, 85

office hours
    of faculty, 79–80
    problems or questions for, 109
outlines, 46, 125
Overbaugh, R., 31

paraphrasing
    active reading as, 45
    metacognitive reading strategy
        as, 40
    from understanding, 30–31
passive student, 10

phrases, 16–17
positive emotions
    faculty influenced by, 79
    learning strategies for, 82–83
    motivation and learning
        influenced by, 73–81
    success from, 74, 88
practice problems. *See* example
    problems
practice tests
    deep learning from, 19
    Quizlet and memorize.com for,
        123, 125
problem solving
    concept application for, 31
    growth mindset from, 70
    metacognition as, 10
    office hours and tutoring for, 109
    working harder *versus*, 11–13
prodigies, 66
professional development, 4
professors. *See* faculty

questions
    answers found by, 44–45
    class attendance for asking, 36
    exams from types of, 97
    preview reading and asking,
        43–45
quizzes
    classes after review of, 110
    mock exams from, 55–56,
        97–98
    study buddy for, 110

reading
    for chapter mapping, 124–25
    comprehension and active, x
    of directions in exams, 98

homework before and after,
51–52
metacognitive strategy for, 40
not learning from, 41
paraphrasing as active, 45
as preview, preparation,
paraphrasing, 40
reading as preview
big picture with, 35
as before class, 109
headings, bold and italic print,
charts as, 42–44
metacognitive reading as, 40
questions before and after, 43–45
recordings
lectures captured in, 50
notes from, 124
reflective questions, 24
remembering
Goldilocks use as, 32
memorization from, 30
responsibility
assistance sought as, 87
as owning actions and results, 86
students changing from fault to, 20
rest. *See* sleep deprivation
review
note gaps filled with, 36
of notes after class, 109
study cycle as, 35

self-talk
motivation influenced by, 83–84
as support, 110
semester calendar
projects, exams, events listed on,
90–91
time management prioritizing,
89–97

shallow learning, 23
sleep deprivation, 85
students experiencing, 75
weekly calendar to avoid, 92
solutions, metacognition for, 10
stress management, 89–99
students, 1
environment as creation of, 83
exercise and sleep lack by, 75
fault to responsibility for, 20
learning for, 6–8
learning strategies unknown by,
x, 7
memorization journey by, 3–5
motivation levers and obstacles
for, 75–76
performance controlled by, 21
in study mode, 26–27
syllabus questions from, 78–79
in teach mode for learning, 54
test mode for, 28–29
study buddy, 57, 110
study cycles
flexible times for, 38
with metacognition, 34
preview, class, review, study, asses,
35
study sessions with, 34–38
weekly schedule for, 92
study guides, 125
studying
Bloom's Taxonomy on, 24–27
learning *versus*, 24–27
as short-term memorization, 25
study cycle as, 35
timers ensuring breaks in, 124
weekly calendar for, 92
study sessions
active learning in, 35, 37

flashcards and mapping in, 37
  with study cycles, 34–38
study time, 109
study tools, 123–25
success, 1
  active learning for, 83–84
  emotions as building, 74, 88
  exercise as supportive of, 85–86
  growth mindset from, 68–69
  learning strategies for, 82–83
  motivation influenced by, 74
  nutrition for, 85
  responsibility taken for, 86
  sleep deprivation and, 85
  work schedule for, 87
Sydnie
  first-semester exam scores of, 81
  learning strategies for, 80–81
  motivation for, 80–81
syllabus
  for faculty expectations, 78–79
  mock exams from, 55
systematic approach, 4

tables of contents, in textbooks,
    49–50
teachers. *See* faculty
teaching
  Cornell requirement of, 4
  as multiple explanations, 28
teach mode, x, 4
  group learning as, 54–55
  learning strategies as, 29
  students and learning in, 54
  test mode *versus*, 27–29
test mode
  students in, 28–29
  teach mode *versus*, 27–29

tests. *See also* practice tests
  comprehension increased with,
    55
  homework as reworked before,
    109
textbooks
  charts, graphs, diagrams, example
    problems in, 47
  faculty knowledge included in, 47
  homework before review of, 109
  metacognitive strategies
    depending on, 49
  sources of, 48
  subject coverage as in, 46–49
  tables of contents and indexes in,
    49–50
time management
  falling behind without, 89–90
  prioritizing needs and wants in,
    96
  semesters prioritized by, 89–97
  stress management from, 89–99
  time protection as, 92–93
timers
  Marinara Timer app as, 124
  study and break times ensured by,
    124
Travis
  metacognition for, 12
  reading strategies for, 41–42
tutoring
  at learning centers, 99
  regular visits for, 109
T Zone seating, 50–51

understanding
  Bloom's Taxonomy as, 23, 30, 31
  Goldilocks preferences as, 32

memorization *versus*, 11
paraphrasing for, 30–31

values, motivation influenced by, 74
vowel exercise, 14–20

Warner, Isiah, 66–67
weekly calendar, 94–95

classes, study, work, social,
    shopping, sleep on, 92
exercise on, 88
study time as days on, 109
working harder
    overload as interfering with, 87
problem solver *versus*, 11–13
workshops, 9, 17–18